COLLINS

Design and Technology Foundation Course

Resistant Materials Systems & Control

Mike Finney
Head of Design and Technology and GNVQ Co-ordinator,
William Farr CofE Comprehensive School Welton

Colin Chapman
Technology Enhancement Programme Adviser

Michael Horsley
Technology Consultant

Collins Educational
An imprint of HarperCollinsPublishers

|CONTENTS

Dedicated to the memory of Mel Peace

Published by Collins Educational
An imprint of HarperCollins*Publishers*
77-85 Fulham Palace Road
London W6 8JB

www.CollinsEducation.com
On-line Support for Schools and Colleges

© HarperCollins*Publishers* 1997

First published 1997
20 19 18 17 16 15 14 13 12 11
ISBN 0 00 327352 0

Mike Finney, Colin Chapman and Michael Horsley assert the moral right
to be identified as the authors of this work.

British Library Cataloguing in Publication Data
A catalogue record for this book is available from the British Library.

Parts of this book have been adapted from material that previously appeared in
Collins CDT Foundation Course, *The Process* and *Techniques and Resources*.

Designed by Ken Vail Graphic Design (production management Chris Williams)
Cover Design by Ken Vail Graphic Design
Cover photograph: Michael Manni Photographic
Illustrated by: Mike Badrocke, Tim Cooke, Sam Denley, Simon Girling & Associates
(Chris Etheridge, Alex Pang, Mike Taylor), Dalton-Jacobs, Ken Vail Graphic Design,
David Lock, Linda Rogers Associates (Ann Baum), Malcolm Ryan
Printed and bound in Hong Kong
Edited by: Alison Walters and Margaret Shepherd
Editorial Assistant: Tamsin Miller
Production: Sue Cashin

WHAT IS DESIGN & TECHNOLOGY?

Design and technology (D&T) is about using a range of materials, skills and knowledge to design and make products. It is an exciting and interesting subject that requires you to develop your ability to solve problems and make quality products. In D&T you learn how to work with different tools and materials, and to understand how everyday things work.

Planning a project

D&T is a subject which allows you to make use of the things learnt in other subjects such as science and mathematics. It enables you to make practical use of the skills and knowledge you gain from those subjects.

Information technology (IT) is an invaluable tool in D&T. It will help you to collect and handle information, design things, present your ideas and make them. It is very difficult to imagine D&T without it.

Some of the materials used in D&T

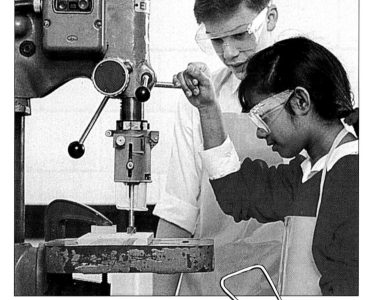

Working on a D&T project

Your D&T work in school will be varied. You will be given tasks which require you to solve a problem by designing and making quality products. You may do things which will enable you to practise your skills or you may have to find out how familiar products are made and how they work. During some of the activities in D&T you will be working on your own, developing your own ideas and skills and learning how to make decisions for yourself. For other projects you will work in groups and learn how to work together as a team.

D&T is a very important part of the world in which we live. It affects our lives in many ways. Imagine what life would be like without the things around us that have been designed and made. Designing and making things creates wealth for us as a nation by providing us with jobs in business and industry. We design, make and sell products to ensure that we enjoy a high standard of living.

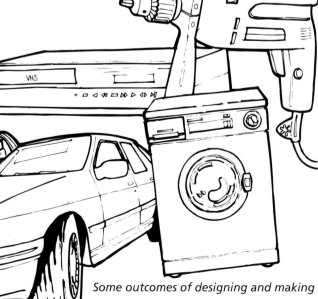

Some outcomes of designing and making

1 DESIGNING

The process of designing and making can be divided into groups of activities. The diagram shown in Fig. 1.1 shows the design process and the stages involved in it. In order to make it easier to understand, the process is shown as a line, but in fact it is more like the circular process shown in Fig. 1.2. Once you have made something and evaluated it, you could go through the whole process again and improve your design.

1 Starting points
Contexts
Identifying needs
Design briefs
Evaluating existing products

2 Generating a design proposal
Drawing up a specification
Sketching and modelling
Ideas
Evaluating ideas
Choosing ideas

3 Planning and making
Product planning
Resource planning
Action planning
Making

4 Evaluating
Final evaluation
Other people's evaluation
Improving your finished product

Fig. 1.1
A linear design process

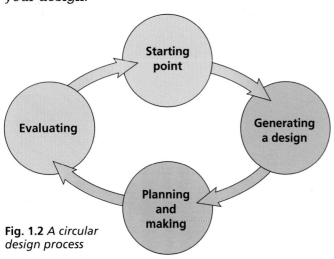

Fig. 1.2 *A circular design process*

Design frameworks

At first, designing might seem to be a complicated activity with many different things to think about, but designing products is not difficult once you know what to do. If you were sent on an errand to a place that you had not been to before you would probably be given a map marked with a route. In D&T you can use a series of design frameworks as a route through the design process. These frameworks will help you to design and make quality products.

At first, the design framework you are given will give you a great deal of help and much of the work will be done for you – you will only have to carry out simple tasks yourself. As you work through the course and develop your designing skills, you will do more of the work yourself. Gradually, you will take control of your work and the design framework will only consist of a series of headings for each part of the project. Fig. 1.3 shows an example of a framework. You can see that a lot of the work has already been done for you.

Problem

For many of you, coming to a new school for the first time can be a strange experience. You will have to face many new problems. Meeting new people, moving around in a much larger school and having to look after your books and belongings.

Identifying your own property can be a problem.

Make a list of the things which might be difficult to identify.

Brief

A brief is a statement or clear sentence that tells other people what you are going to do.

Complete the following brief:

I am going to design and make

Analysis

Finding out more about what you have to do is known as **analysing the problem**.

Answer the following questions in full sentences.

1. What job will my finished design have to do?

2. List the different materials you will be able to use.

3. Write down the maximum size that your project should not exceed.

4. How much will it cost to make?

5. How much time will you have to make and evaluate your design?

6. Is there anything else you need to know in order to finish the project?

William Farr
D&T

Name	Form	D&T Teacher

Fig. 1.3 *A design framework*

Starting points

There are several ways of starting to design things. These starting points will change as your designing skills develop.

Design briefs ➡

You may be given a brief which will tell you what you have to do. You will need to think carefully about the brief and try to work out exactly what is required. Professional designers often work in this way and are given a brief by their customer or client.

STANLEY **STANLEY TOOLS**
WOODSIDE   SHEFFIELD   S3 9PD   ENGLAND

FROM Marketing Dept.   TO Product Development

SUBJECT Stanley Mini Knife.
        New Product Proposal No 5-71

Brief-
To design a new pocket knife which will make use of the existing 'slimknife' blade.

Specification.
1. The blade must be fully retractable.
2. It must be safe to operate.
3. It must make use of the 5901 blade
4. The knife body maybe constructed by die casting, pressing or plastic moulding.
5. The blade must be easily replaceable - preferably without the use of tools. (eg coin slotted screw.)

Fig. 1.4 *A design brief*

Fig. 1.5 *Working from a context*

⬅ Contexts

Sometimes you will be given a context or a situation to work from. You will be expected to investigate the context, work out what is required and write your own design brief. The context might describe a particular problem for you to think about, and you will be required to design something which will solve the problem.

Identifying needs ➡

Working from a context or a situation often involves looking at other people's needs and requirements. Everyone has needs – as human beings we all need air, water, food, warmth and shelter. These are our basic needs, but in addition to these we have more, depending upon our on situation. People with disabilities have special needs, people might have particular needs which come from the job they do or a situation they find themselves in. Identifying these needs is a good starting point for designing.

Fig. 1.6 *Different needs*

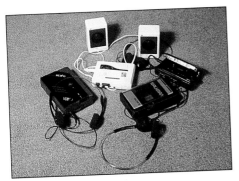

Fig. 1.7 *Evaluating existing products*

Study Fig. 1.5 in detail. Write down as many opportunities for designing as you can find.

⬅ Evaluating existing products

Working from existing products is another way to start designing. This involves looking very carefully at products, finding out how they are made and how they work, and working out whether they are successful or not. You will need to consider if it would be possible to improve the design of the product or find another way of solving the problem. This is known as evaluating existing products. Much of the design work done in industry involves re-designing existing products.

Generating design proposals

Investigating

Looking very carefully at something or studying it in detail is called investigating in D&T. This means finding out as much as you can about a situation, problem or product. For instance, you will have to investigate the design brief or the context in order to find out what you need to do. When identifying needs, you will have to gain a thorough understanding of the needs of others before you can begin to solve problems for them. Investigating will involve you in collecting information from many different sources. First-hand information gathered by talking to people or making observations is known as information from a **primary source**. Information that you have got out of books or that has been gathered by others is said to come from a **secondary source**.

Fig. 1.8 *Investigating*

Brainstorming ➡

If you are working in a group you may find it useful to have a **brainstorming** session. This is a good way of finding out other people's ideas about a topic. When you organise a brainstorming session you may find it useful to follow the simple rules shown in Fig. 1.9.

Brainstorming rules

1 Choose someone to record the ideas that are suggested. They can be written on a flip chart, a chalkboard or a large sheet of paper.

2 Write down everything that the group can think of that is related to the topic. Remember that any idea is worth writing down at this stage.

3 Don't be tempted to discuss the ideas as you think of them. Write them down first and discuss them later.

4 Try to prevent the brainstorming session from going on too long. Set a time in which to work – 15 to 20 minutes should be long enough.

Fig. 1.9

⬅ Spider diagrams

Spider diagrams are a useful way of recording a brainstorming session. Begin by writing the topic in the centre of the page and then write each idea around it. You could draw a line to link each idea to the topic. This will help you later if it becomes a large or complicated diagram. Allow the diagram to grow as ideas are recorded.

Fig. 1.10 *An example of a spider diagram*

Identifying constraints ➡

When carrying out your investigation it is important for you to think about all the things that may affect your product, such as how much time and how much money are available. These things are called **constraints** and they have an important effect on the outcome of your work. Other constraints will include the materials that are available and your level of ability (it may be necessary for you to learn new skills in order to make your product). As you think carefully about your task you will be able to identify relevant constraints. They will vary in importance, depending on the nature of the task. The constraints affecting the design of a child's toy are shown in the diagram in Fig. 1.11.

Fig. 1.11 *Constraints on the design of a child's toy*

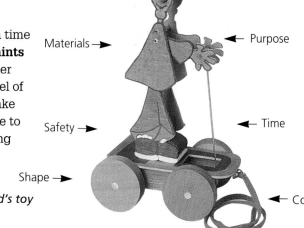

Drawing up a specification

Criteria ➡

Once you have identified the constraints affecting your product you can work out the criteria that your product needs to meet. A criterion is something that the final design must do. For example, one of the constraints affecting toy products is safety. Therefore, one of the criteria for a child's toy is that it must be safe.

Fig. 1.12 *Thinking about criteria*

Specification

My toy design for young children should:

- be attractive
- not be too expensive
- be easy for me to make
- be made in the time allowed
- be colourful
- be safe
- be made from the materials available

Fig. 1.13 *A simple specification*

Specification ➡

When you have worked out the criteria that your product needs to satisfy, you should make a list of them. This forms your **specification**. You can write either a simple or a detailed specification. A simple specification lists the criteria in any order of importance. A more detailed specification gives more information, and divides the criteria into two groups – essential criteria and desirable criteria. **Essential criteria** are the criteria that your product must satisfy. **Desirable criteria** are the criteria that your product should satisfy, if possible. Specifications are an important part of designing because they provide a check list against which you can review your ideas as you are working. They also give you something against which to evaluate your ideas, design proposals and your finished product.

Specification

Essential criteria

My toy design for young children must:

1. Be safe for young children to play with. It must have no sharp edges or loose parts.
2. Be attractive and interesting for young children.
3. Be made of wood and plastic.
4. Be made in six weeks.

Desirable criteria

My toy design for young children should:

1. Cost less than £5.00 in materials.
2. Be painted and varnished.
3. Be possible for me to make by myself.

Fig. 1.14 *A more detailed specification*

Ideas

Once you have drawn up a specification the next stage in generating a design proposal is to start thinking about ideas or solutions to the problem. The aim is to begin with a number of ideas and develop some of them into a design proposal. Fig. 1.15 shows these stages of the design process.

Sources of inspiration ➡

Designers get their ideas from a variety of different sources. Leonardo da Vinci (1452–1519) is said to have studied the flight of birds when he was designing his flying machines (see Fig. 1.16). Many other designers have been inspired by nature. Because it is difficult to think of something completely new, designers often begin work by looking at existing products. Many successful designs have been developed from earlier existing designs.

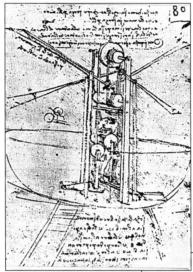

Fig. 1.16 *Da Vinci's ideas for the design of a helicopter*

SPECIFICATION
IDEAS
EVALUATING IDEAS
CHOOSING AN IDEA
DESIGN PROPOSAL

Fig. 1.15

Use your specification ➡

Don't be too worried if you do not feel inspired as you try to think of ideas. The specification will help you because it provides you with a detailed list of the criteria that your finished product should satisfy. Think about each of the criteria in turn and try to keep them in mind as you are working. At this stage you should be trying to produce as many ideas as you can. You should even include the silliest ideas, as they may be of use to you later. Ask yourself questions as you work, and try to be as open minded as possible. Try to remember to review your ideas and compare them with the specification as you continue to work.

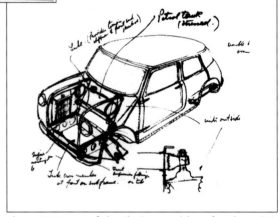

Fig. 1.17 *Some of the designer's ideas for the Mini*

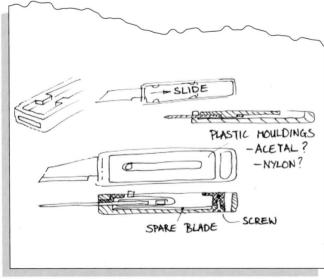

Fig. 1.18 *Design ideas for a small modelling knife*

⬅ Recording and presenting your ideas

Once your ideas start to flow you need to record them before they are forgotten. Ideas are best recorded quickly and then worked on and developed later. It is possible to make notes of your ideas but you will probably find it easier to draw them.

Modelling is another way of recording ideas but it can sometimes take a lot longer than drawing.

Whatever method you choose, your work must be easy to understand and well presented. Your teacher and those working with you in groupwork must be able to understand the ideas that you are trying to communicate. The following pages will help you with using graphics as a method of communicating ideas.

Using graphics

Graphics are a vital part of D&T. The word 'graphics' describes the type of drawings that are made during the design process. Design drawings are used to explain thoughts and ideas – they can do this more clearly than words alone can. Graphics are used to show what something will look like when it has been made. They can also give instructions and describe how to do something, such as how to make a product or carry out a task.

Graphic media

Graphic media are anything that can be used to create a drawing, a painting or a picture. Pencils, pens, markers, paint, cameras and some computer software packages are all examples of graphic media. You do not need to buy expensive and complicated drawing equipment in order to be able to draw well. Pencils and paper are all you need to begin with.

Fig. 1.19 *A range of graphic media*

Paper ➡

There are many different types of paper available, ranging from very expensive handmade paper to the cheaper, more common papers such as newsprint. (This is the paper on which most of our newspapers are printed.) For most of your drawing work you will probably use **cartridge paper**. This is excellent for general drawing and is particularly good for pencil and ink drawings. Many designers do their rough work on thin paper called **layout paper**. This is a white drawing paper which is thin enough to be used to trace drawings through.

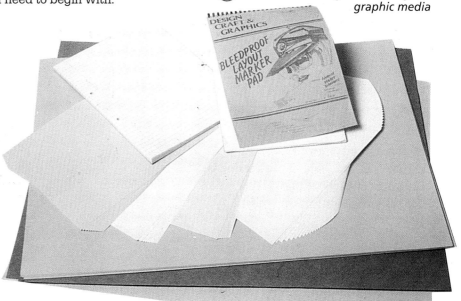

Paper is available in a variety of different sizes and weights. It can be bought in a range of sizes known as the 'A' series. A0 is the largest and A6 the smallest. The sizes of paper most used in schools are A4 and A3. Fig. 1.21 shows the paper sizes. A sheet of A3 paper is the same size as two sheets of A4 paper placed side by side. The largest size of paper in the A series, A0, measures 1189 mm × 841 mm – the area of one square metre.

The weight of a sheet of paper is a guide to how thick it is. The thicker the paper, the more it weighs. Thin layout paper weighs 45 gsm (grams per square metre) while good quality cartridge paper might weigh 120 gsm.

Fig. 1.20 *Some of the many types of paper*

Find three types of paper, of different weights and textures. Using hard and soft pencils see how many types of marks and tones you can draw. What differences are there between the papers? Which is the best for pencil drawing?

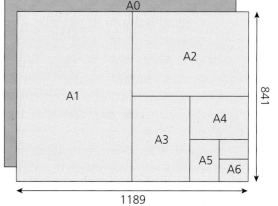

Fig. 1.21 *The 'A' series paper sizes*

Pencils

Traditional pencils consist of a wooden case glued around a graphite core, as shown in Fig. 1.22. They are available in many different grades, ranging from very hard to very soft. Fig. 1.23 shows the range of pencil grades available. Hard pencils produce a thin grey line, while soft pencils produce a thicker black line. You will only need two pencils to begin with; a 2H to give you a fine, light line; and an HB to give a softer, darker line.

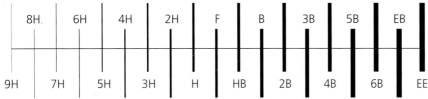

8H		6H		4H		2H		F		B		3B		5B		EB	
9H	7H		5H		3H		H		HB		2B		4B		6B		EE

Fig. 1.23 *Pencil grades*

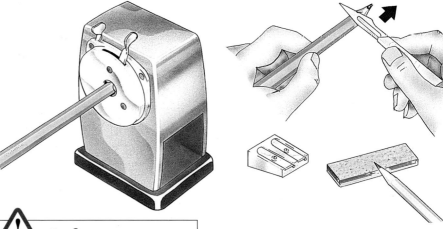

Fig. 1.22 *Traditional pencils*

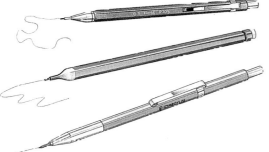

Fig. 1.24 *Clutch pencils*

Clutch pencils, like the ones shown in Fig. 1.24, look similar to plastic biros but contain leads instead of ink. Fine-lead clutch pencils have very thin leads made of polymer and graphite. They are usually half a millimetre thick but can be as thin as 0.3mm. Clutch pencils always give the same thickness of line and do not need to be sharpened.

Sharpening Pencils

Pencils need to kept sharp. There may be a sharpener fixed to a desk in your classroom or you may have a small sharpener of your own. It is a good idea to use a small piece of glass paper to keep a sharp point on your pencil.

Pencils can also be sharpened with a craft knife, but take care when doing this. Always cut away from yourself (see Fig. 1.25).

> ⚠️ **Safety**
> Always cut away from your body when using a knife as a sharpener.

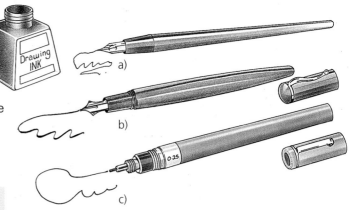

Fig. 1.25 *Pencil sharpeners*

Using ink

Ink is another useful medium for sketching your ideas, although it is more difficult to erase your mistakes. You can draw with ink straight from the bottle using a dip pen. Drawing pens fitted with an ink cartridge are less messy but many people prefer to use a fine-line pen. Fine-line pens are available as disposable fibre tips or as refillable technical pens which have a hollow metal needle as a tip. Ball pens can also be used, but it is a good idea only to use ones with black ink in them.

> *On a piece of scrap paper, experiment with a 2H and an HB pencil. Use each pencil to draw a series of lines and try shading with them. Which pencil gives a darker line? Which pencil feels harder when you draw with it?*

Fig. 1.26 *Ink pens: a) a dip pen; b) a cartridge drawing pen; c) a technical pen*

Freehand sketching

Freehand sketching is a very good way of recording and presenting your ideas quickly and freely. Ideas can be sketched in a variety of different media, ranging from traditional pencils to ball pens or fine-line pens. Sketch lightly and quickly. Don't worry if you go wrong – you can either draw over it or rub it out later. Your aim should be to get your ideas down on paper as quickly as you can. Fig. 1.27 shows a sheet of ideas sketched by a pupil for a child's toy.

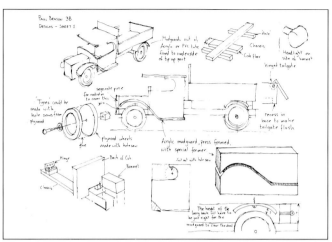

Fig. 1.27 *Freehand sketches*

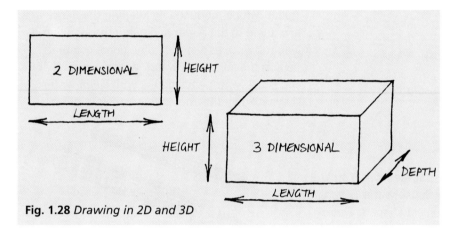

Fig. 1.28 *Drawing in 2D and 3D*

◀ *Sketching in 3D*

Some of the ideas in Fig. 1.27 have been sketched in **two dimensions** (2D) and others in **three dimensions** (3D). Two-dimensional drawings show only two basic measurements (dimensions) – height and width. A three-dimensional drawing shows three basic measurements – height, width and depth (see Fig. 1.28). Three-dimensional drawings show more information and make your ideas look more solid and realistic.

Crating ➡

When learning to sketch in 3D, it is a good idea to try to imagine the objects that you want to draw inside a three-dimensional box. Draw the boxes very lightly first and then draw in the object, using the box as a guide (Fig. 1.29). This technique is known as crating and will help you to draw in 3D.

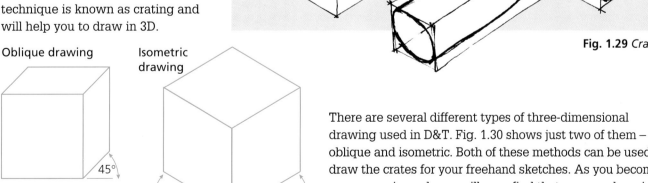

Fig. 1.29 *Crating*

Oblique drawing

Isometric drawing

Fig. 1.30 *Oblique and isometric drawing*

45°

30°   30°

There are several different types of three-dimensional drawing used in D&T. Fig. 1.30 shows just two of them – oblique and isometric. Both of these methods can be used to draw the crates for your freehand sketches. As you become more experienced, you will soon find that you can draw in 3D without using crates.

1   Practise crating by drawing some of the hand tools in your workshop – hammers, mallets, chisels and screwdrivers could all be drawn using crating.

2   Choose a familiar box-shaped object, such as a pencil box, and make a freehand oblique drawing of it.

Using colour

When you have sketched your ideas, in either pencil or ink, you can think about adding colour to them. A wide range of colouring materials is available for you to use on your drawings. The main reasons for colouring your sketches in D&T are either to draw attention to parts of the drawing, or to make a drawing of a finished product look more realistic.

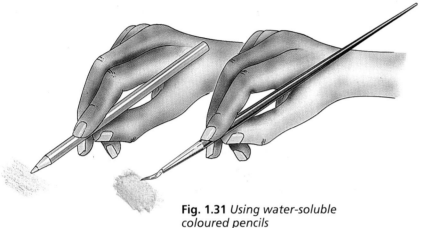

Fig. 1.31 *Using water-soluble coloured pencils*

◀ *Coloured pencils*

You are probably already familiar with coloured pencils as they are one of the easiest ways of applying colour to a drawing. A solid area of colour can be produced by keeping the pencil at a low angle to the paper and using the side of the lead rather than just the point. Some coloured pencils are soluble in water, which means that if you brush your pencil marks with clean water they will give the effect of watercolour paint.

Marker pens ➡

There are two kinds of marker pens used for graphic work. You are already familiar with the felt-tipped pens which use water-based ink. The tips of these pens are either rounded or chisel-shaped. Water-based ink takes a minute or two to dry, so you must be careful not to smudge it. The other type of marker can usually be recognised by its smell. It uses spirit-based ink which dries very quickly, and is often known as a graphic or studio marker. Spirit-based markers have a much wider range of colours than the water-based type and most of them can be refilled when they run out. You will need to work quickly with this type of marker otherwise the ink will dry and leave a striped effect on your work. Sometimes the ink spreads out over the outlines of your drawing or soaks through the paper. To stop this happening you will need a special bleed-proof paper. Ask your teacher about this.

Fig. 1.32 *Marker pens*

⚠ Safety

Always use spirit-based markers in a well-ventilated area and avoid breathing in the fumes.

Poster paint and watercolours ➡

Poster paint and gouache are opaque forms of water-based paint. They can be used when you want to paint over your work so that the drawing does not show through. Watercolour is used to provide thin transparent washes of colour which allow the drawing to show through. Washes can be built up in layers to strengthen or darken the colours, as shown in Fig. 1.35. Remember that working with wet media such as watercolour will require you to stretch your paper before use to prevent it from wrinkling and distorting when it gets wet. Fig. 1.33 shows you how to do this.

Fig. 1.33 *Stretching paper before using wet media*

1 Wet paper thoroughly

2 Drain off excess water

3 Stick to a clean board with gummed tape and allow to dry.

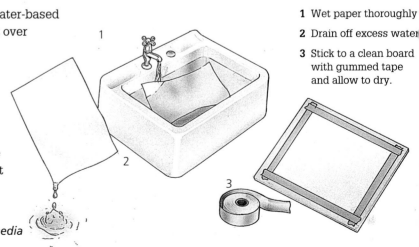

Highlighting ➡

When you have completed a sheet of sketches you can draw attention to some of the ideas by **highlighting** them. This is done either by applying colour around the idea as shown in Fig. 1.34, or by putting colour on the idea itself (Fig. 1.35).

Colouring an idea in this way allows you to show it as a three-dimensional object. The form of the object can easily be seen by the effect of light and shade. Take care not to overdo the colour – too much can spoil a drawing and will not improve it. Avoid using really bright colours. The best colours to use on sketches are earthy colours, such as browns, yellows and greens.

Fig. 1.34 *Colour applied around the idea*

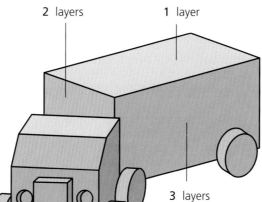

2 layers   1 layer

3 layers

Fig. 1.35 *Colour applied to the idea*

⬅ Rendering

Colour can be used to give an impression of the type of material used to make something (**rendering**). The drawing of the boat in Fig. 1.36 has been rendered in this way and clearly shows that it is constructed from wood and acrylic. Rendering is not difficult to do and can look very effective. Study the materials yourself first, to get an understanding of them, and then try to simplify them. Try it with a piece of wood. Draw the shape in pencil and shade it with a yellow or light brown coloured pencil. Then draw in the details of the grain using a dark brown coloured pencil. When rendering acrylic or metal you will need to look carefully at the reflections on the surface and include them in your drawing.

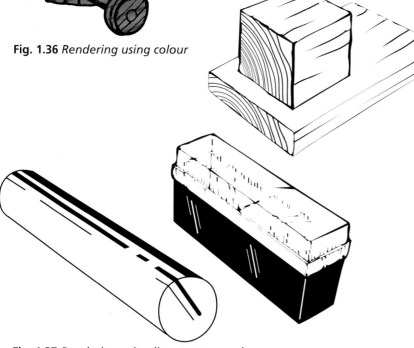

Fig. 1.36 *Rendering using colour*

You can also use **line**, **texture** and **tone** to suggest the materials that an object is made from (Fig. 1.37). Try these techniques for yourself – the methods are simple and the effects are impressive.

1 Draw two or three rectangular blocks in perspective and practise putting on a thin wash of colour. Think about where the light is coming from and make the shaded areas darker by building up layers of wash. The area nearest the light should be a lighter tone.

2 Draw a series of cubes and then use your graphic skills to make them look as if they are made out of different materials, such as wood, metal, glass and plastic.

Fig. 1.37 *Rendering using line, texture and tone*

Evaluating ideas

*Once you have produced a range of ideas, you can begin the process of choosing the most suitable to develop further. This is done by **evaluating** your ideas. Evaluating is a very important part of the designing process. At this stage careful evaluation will ensure that what you design solves the problem and fulfils the criteria set out in the specification. It is very easy to stray off the topic and design things that do not really solve the problem if you do not evaluate your work carefully.*

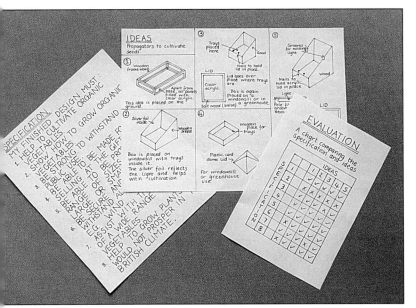

Fig. 1.38

In order to evaluate your ideas look at each idea carefully and compare it with the specification. Does it do all of the things that the specification said it should? Compare each idea with the specification in turn and you will be able to see which idea is worth developing further. Don't worry if more than one idea is suitable. You can develop more than one idea and then evaluate them again at a later stage.

A simple and effective way of beginning an evaluation is to make a chart to record your results on like the one shown in Fig. 1.38. List the ideas across the top of the grid and the criteria from the specification down the side. If the idea conforms with the criteria, put a tick in the box; if it doesn't, put a cross in the box. You will be able to see very easily which ideas are worth developing by simply counting up the ticks.

Choosing an idea ➡

When you have completed your chart you can then look very carefully at the ideas that satisfy the criteria of the specification. Ask yourself a number of questions about the wider design considerations which may affect you and your work. Fig. 1.39 should give you some idea of the type of questions. When you have done this you should be able to choose one or more ideas for the design of your product. The chosen ideas are known as **design proposals**.

Ask yourself ...

Which of my ideas do I like the best?

Will my product harm anyone or anything?

Will my product be environmentally friendly?

Will my product look good?

Will I have to pay for the materials?

Will my product be expensive to make?

How will I finance my product?

Have I the ability to make my product or will I need help from other people?

Fig. 1.39

Developing the chosen idea

Before you can begin to make your chosen idea there are many things that you still need to consider. This stage is known as developing the chosen idea and it is a very important part of the designing process. Your ideas are modified and start to become real objects.

Function ➡

The products that you design must solve the problems set out in your specification. You need to ensure that your idea fulfils its function and does what it is meant to do. Check your work against the specification as your idea develops. If it is an electronic, pneumatic or mechanical product you may need to 'model' it to test out the idea to see if it works.

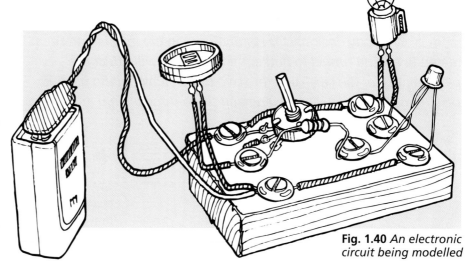

Fig. 1.40 *An electronic circuit being modelled*

Size and shape ➡

A clear understanding of size, shape and form is very important. It is sometimes difficult to imagine the size of something without making a full-size drawing or model. If your product is to come into contact with people then you will need to collect information about their average sizes. This is known as **anthropometric data** (Fig. 1.41) and is used by designers when designing furniture, cars, trains and buses, etc.

Materials ➡

You must consider which materials will be used and how your product will be constructed. Find out what materials are available and then use the most appropriate. It will help you if you have an understanding of the properties of materials in order to know how to use them. For example, you may need to know how to shape, bend or join them. Chapters 2 and 3 (pages 30–65) look at materials and their properties.

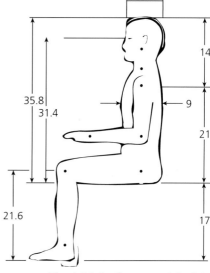

Fig. 1.41 *Anthropometric data*

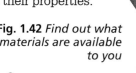

Fig. 1.42 *Find out what materials are available to you*

 Safety

You must consider safety at all times when developing an idea. It is the designer's responsibility to make products that are as safe as possible and will not harm people or the environment. There are very strict **safety standards** in Great Britain which designers and manufacturers must follow. Always aim to produce a safe product.

Appearance

The visual appearance of a product is very important. Designers aim to produce attractive products that work well. The visual qualities that make things look attractive are known as **aesthetics**. It is important that you should always aim to make your products as visually attractive as possible. Think carefully about what the product will look like. Will it be painted, varnished or polished? Always aim to produce a quality product.

Modelling and presentation drawing

Modelling is an excellent way of developing your ideas – we have already seen how circuits and mechanisms can be modelled to see if they work. Modelling your products gives you a clear idea of what your finished design will look like. Architects make scale models to see what their buildings will look like. Designers often make full-size models. Car body designs, for instance, are made in clay and then tested in a wind tunnel to find out if the shape will affect the performance of the car. There are two forms of modelling used in D&T, two-dimensional modelling and three-dimensional modelling.

Fig. 1.43 *An architect's scale model*

◀ *Two-dimensional modelling*

Two-dimensional modelling is often used to represent electronic or mechanical systems. **Block diagrams** can be drawn to represent the system and sometimes **flow diagrams** are used to show a sequence of actions. A computer can also be used to make a two-dimensional model. Software is available to model electronic circuits and test designs.

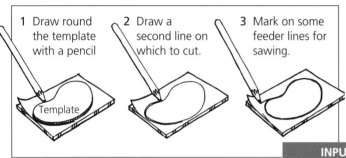

Fig. 1.44 *A block diagram for a system and a flow diagram for marking out acrylic.*

INPUT	CONTROL	OUTPUT
Needs to sense when it goes dark.	Needs to switch on the output when the input senses dark.	Needs to light up when the control switches it on.

Presentation drawings ➡

Presentation drawings are another form of two-dimensional modelling. They are high-quality representations drawn to make an idea look as realistic as possible. The drawing is rendered in colour using marker pens, coloured pencils or watercolour.

Perspective drawing

There are two main types of perspective drawing used in D&T, **single-point perspective** and **two-point perspective**. Both can be used for presentation drawings, but two-point perspective is the most commonly used because it is more lifelike. Perspective drawing uses the fact that to our eyes the lines of objects going away into the distance appear to meet at a vanishing point somewhere on the horizon. Fig. 1.46 shows a cube drawn in single-point perspective. Two-point perspective allows us to draw objects at an angle rather than straight on. This means that the horizontal lines will recede in two different directions, converging at two different vanishing points. Fig. 1.47 shows how to draw a cube in two-point perspective. Presentation drawings are usually begun by drawing crates, as shown in Fig. 1.29 on page 13, except that the crates are drawn using two-point perspective.

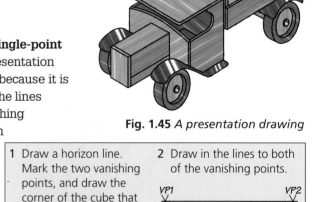

Fig. 1.45 *A presentation drawing*

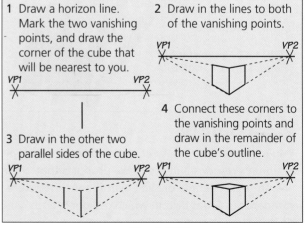

1 Draw a horizon line. Mark the two vanishing points, and draw the corner of the cube that will be nearest to you.

2 Draw in the lines to both of the vanishing points.

3 Draw in the other two parallel sides of the cube.

4 Connect these corners to the vanishing points and draw in the remainder of the cube's outline.

Fig. 1.47 *Two-point perspective*

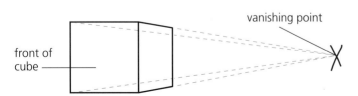

Fig. 1.46 *Single-point perspective*

Three-dimensional modelling ➡

Three-dimensional modelling is a very useful way of developing and testing your ideas. It will also give you some idea of the size and shape of your final design and provide you with something on which you can base your working drawings.

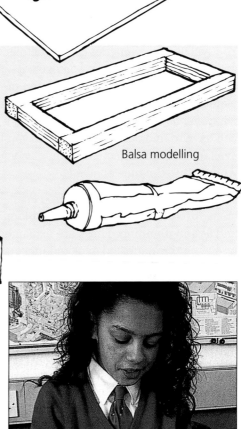

Fig. 1.48 *Modelling tools*

Modelling materials ➡

Models can be made from a variety of materials. Card, balsawood, Plasticine and wire are all suitable. Even materials that would normally be thrown away can be used, such as off-cuts, wood shavings, plastic containers and newspaper.

You will need some simple tools for model making – a sharp modelling knife and steel safety ruler are essential. A junior hacksaw will also be needed to cut small pieces of wood and metal. Remember to hold the work securely when you are cutting. When you are using a knife, always cut on a cutting board and take care not to damage the work surface. You may need to refer to the chapter on working with materials on pages 38 to 65.

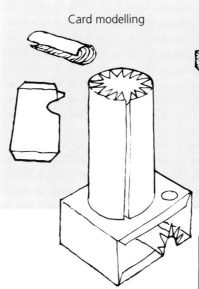

Card modelling

Balsa modelling

Fig. 1.49 *Some modelling materials*

Modelling kits ➡

Modelling kits can be very useful when you are working on mechanical projects that involve moving parts. Simple models can be quickly constructed using kits such as Lego or Fisher Technic. It is a good idea to keep a record of your model by taking a photograph or making a sketch of it. You will probably have to dismantle your model and return the parts to the kit at some time.

Fig. 1.50 *Working with a modelling kit*

⬅ Presentation models

In D&T, a presentation model is made when it is impossible to make the actual product. It shows as clearly as possible what the finished product would look like. You may need to make a presentation model if you are re-designing or re-styling an existing industry-based product.

Fig. 1.51 *A presentation model*

Planning

Planning is a very important part of the design process. Careful planning will enable you to turn your ideas into reality (realisation). Planning your project thoroughly will help to prevent you from making mistakes and wasting both materials and time.

You will need to work out certain details of your chosen design before you make it – for example, how big it will be, what sort of materials and equipment you will need and what will be the best way of producing it. You will have to find out how much time you have available for the project and then plan your work within the time allowed.

Planning can be divided into three main areas: **product planning**, **resource planning** and **action planning**. These are explained briefly on this page and explored in more detail in the rest of the chapter (pages 22–24).

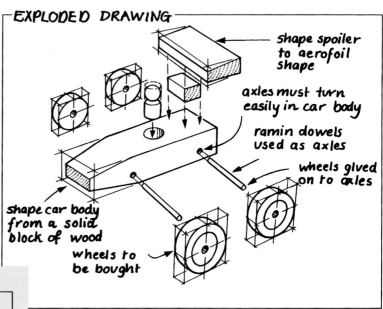

Fig. 1.52 *An exploded drawing*

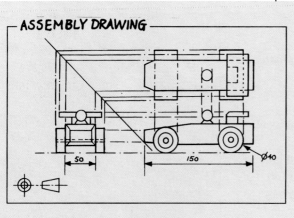

Fig. 1.53 *An assembly drawing*

← Product planning

Working drawings are used to plan and organise the making of a product. They enable you to think about the size of the parts of the product and the way in which they will be fitted together. Figs 1.52 and 1.53 show examples of working drawings.

Resource planning ➡

It is important to work out exactly what materials and parts are required to make your product. It is, therefore, useful to make a list of the resources you will need. This will also show you which materials and parts you will have to order. The list can be used to work out the material cost of your product.

TOY PROJECT: PARTS LIST

Part	Material	Size(mm)	No.
body	softwood	150x50x30	1
wheels	softwood	Ø40x15	4
axles	dowel	Ø6x80	2
driver	softwood	Ø15x30	1
spoiler	softwood	70x30x10	1
support	softwood	30x20x15	1

Fig. 1.54 *A parts list, used to plan resources*

TOY PROJECT: ACTION PLAN

1. Cut out the main parts
2. Cut material for wheels
3. Turn wheels on lathe
4. Drill holes in body
5. Paint or stain
6. Glue together
7. Varnish to give a good shine to the surface

← Action planning

Before you start to make anything, it is important to work out the best way of going about it. Which part do you need to make first? You may need to wait for glue or paint to dry before you can continue. Have you considered this?

Fig. 1.55 *An action plan for making a toy car*

Drawing with instruments

So far, most of your drawing has been done freehand, which is the ideal way of getting your ideas down on paper quickly. The drawings you make at the planning stage, however, are better drawn with instruments because they need to be accurate.

To draw with instruments you will need a drawing board and tee-square, or a special drawing table with a parallel motion fitted to it (this is a wide ruler which is kept at 90° to the edge of the board and is able to slide up and down over the paper) as shown in Fig. 1.56. If you are using a board and tee-square, you must keep the square pressed firmly up to the edge of the board, so that your lines will be horizontal and parallel.

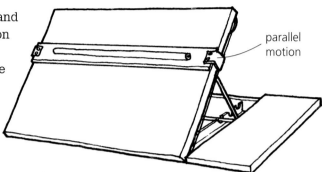

parallel motion

Fig. 1.56

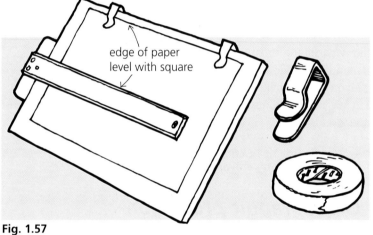

edge of paper level with square

Fig. 1.57

Before starting to draw, you must secure the paper firmly to the board by using special spring clips or tape. Level the paper against the edge of the square or the parallel motion before securing it as shown in Fig. 1.57. You will need two set squares; one with angles of 30, 60 and 90°; and another with 45 and 90°. The set squares are set against the edge of the tee-square to draw lines at various angles (Fig. 1.58). Some angles will need to be drawn with a protractor as it is not possible to draw every angle with a set square.

If you need to draw accurate, neat circles, you will need a pair of compasses. Ordinary school compasses are quite adequate for this, but special draughter's compasses will enable you to be more accurate, especially when you are drawing small circles.

Keep your pencils sharp and remember to begin the drawing with a 2H pencil first and then draw over the lines of the objects with your HB pencil.

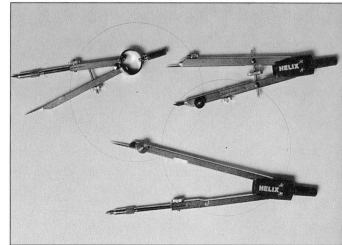

Fig. 1.59 *Different types of compasses*

tee square

Fig. 1.58

Set up your board and level the paper. Using instruments, draw a series of parallel lines at the following angles: 30°, 60°, 45° and 90°. Don't forget to practise drawing horizontal lines as well, especially if you are using a board and tee square.

Working drawings

Once you have formed your design proposal you will need to think very carefully about how you are going to make your design. You must make a number of decisions – for example, how big the product will be, what materials and equipment will be used to make it, how it will be made and what sort of finish it will have. The models and drawings of your design proposal can be used to help you to make these decisions. This information can then be translated into drawings called **working drawings**. These show all the information needed for someone to be able to make a product. You need to remember that, in industry, the person who designs a product is not always the person who will make it.

Fig. 1.60
A polystyrene model is used to help plan the making of a product

Planning is important in schoolwork when you are working with different materials and specialist equipment, but it is even more important in the manufacturing industry. Industrial products are not usually made entirely by one person – the individual parts are made by many different people. Parts are often made in factories in different parts of the country and, sometimes, even in different parts of the world.

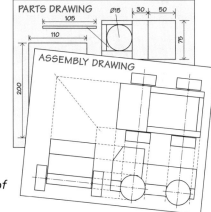

Fig. 1.61 *Examples of working drawings*

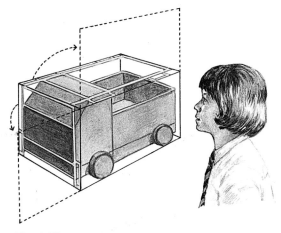

Fig. 1.62a

◀ *Orthographic projection*

Many designers use a system of drawing called **orthographic projection**. Drawings done in this way show the product from different angles so that every detail of the design is shown.

Two types of orthographic projection can be used: **first angle projection** and **third angle projection**. First angle projection can be more difficult to understand so it is simpler to use third angle projection for your working drawings.

Third angle projection

To understand the layout of third angle projection drawings you have to imagine that the object to be drawn is inside a glass box. The view of the object as seen from one angle is then projected on to the glass as shown in Fig. 1.62a. If you imagine unfolding the box in the direction of the arrows, it would look like the drawing in Fig. 1.62b. This shows the side elevation, the front elevation and the plan view of the object.

Choose a familiar object and use drawing instruments to make a very accurate third angle drawing of it. The object can be anything from a watch to a small domestic appliance, or even a small piece of furniture.

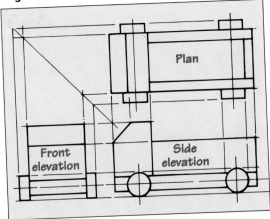

Fig. 1.62b

Parts drawings ➡

If a product consists of several different parts, it is a good idea to make a **parts drawing**. Each part is drawn in orthographic projection, clearly showing its size. The parts drawing contains enough information for each individual part to be made. Fig. 1.63 shows the parts drawing for a wooden lorry, designed for a child's toy project.

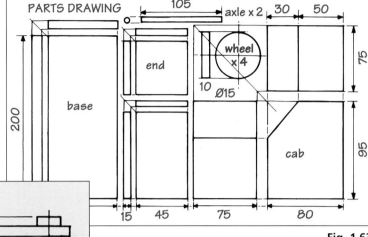

Fig. 1.63

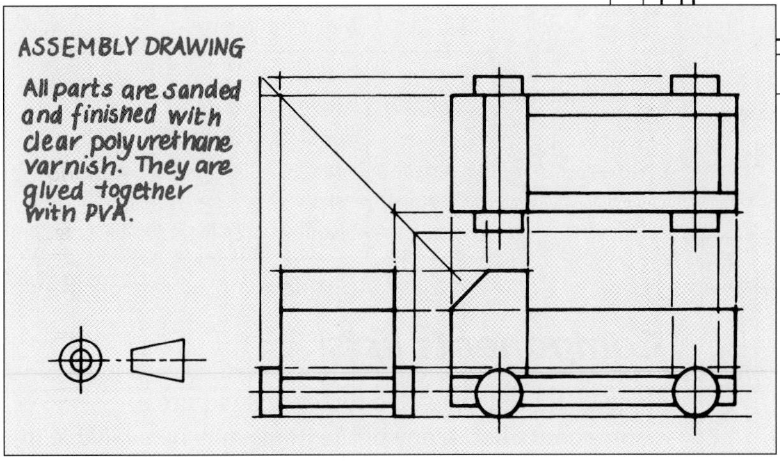

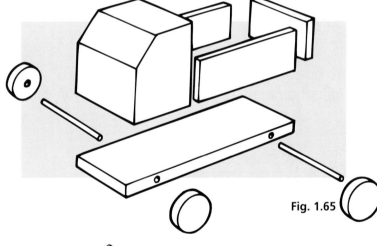

Fig. 1.64

⬅ Assembly drawings

In order to show how the component parts fit together, an **assembly drawing** is made (Fig. 1.64). This shows the final assembled product with all its parts in place. Like the parts drawing, it is drawn using orthographic projection showing three views of the product. Assembly drawings provide enough information for someone to assemble the product.

Exploded drawings ➡

Another way of showing how a product is assembled is to use an **exploded drawing** (Fig. 1.65). If you look in car or motorcycle repair manuals you will find many examples of exploded drawings. Instructions for objects that you have to put together yourself, such as furniture, often use this type of drawing.

Exploded drawings can be very useful when you want to show how something is assembled. They will help you to plan the making of your product.

Fig. 1.65

Sections ➡

Sometimes it is necessary to show what an object looks like inside, in order to understand how it is made. Dotted or broken lines are sometimes used on drawings to show things that you cannot see. Drawings can become very confusing if too many dotted lines are used so it is often better to make a **section drawing** of the object instead.

A section drawing shows an object that has been 'cut' to show what is happening inside. The parts that have actually been cut through are shown by diagonal lines drawn on them (Fig. 1.66). These lines are known as hatching.

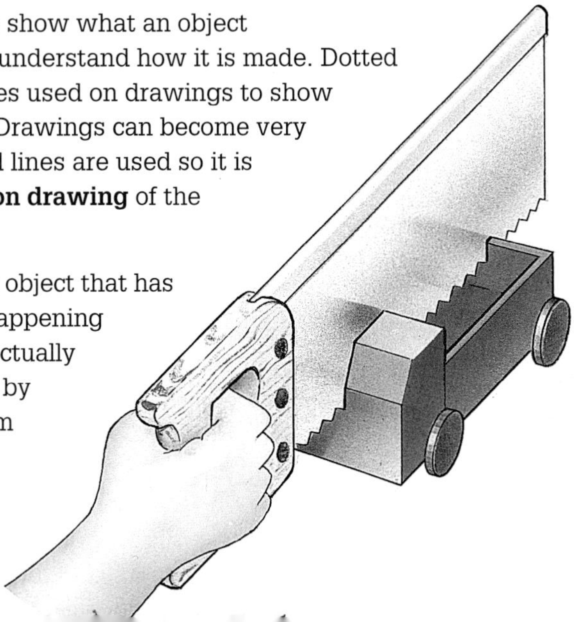

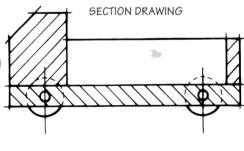

Fig. 1.66

Resource planning

Before you can begin to make your chosen design, it is important that you make a list of everything you will need. This is not difficult if you have made a working drawing of your product or a detailed plan of what you are going to do. The type of list you make will vary according to the project that you are doing. You will be able to use it to find out the material cost of your finished product. You can use either price lists or a computer database to work this out.

Parts lists ➡

Fig. 1.67 shows the **parts list** for the toy racing car shown on page 20. From the list, it is possible to work out exactly how much material is needed and which parts, if any, can be bought ready-made.

Quantity	Component	Cost	✓
1	PCB board 70 × 50		
1	BFY51 transistor		
1	1K resistor		
1	ORP 12 LDR		
1	bulb holder		
1	MES bulb 6V 60mA		
1	PP3 battery connector		
1	PP3 battery		

PCB layout

No. Part	Material	Size	No. of
1. body	beech	150 × 50×30	1
2. wheels	beech	Ø40 × 15	4
3. axles	dowel	Ø6 × 80	2
4. driver	beech	Ø15 × 30	1
5. spoiler	beech	70 × 30 × 10	1
6. support	beech	30 × 20 × 15	1

Fig. 1.67

Components lists

Projects that involve electronics will require a **components list**. Many of the items may be available in school, but you may need to order specialised components.

Fig. 1.68 *A components list*

Action Planning

To make sure that you make the best use of your time, energy and resources, it is important to make a plan of action that you can follow during the making process.

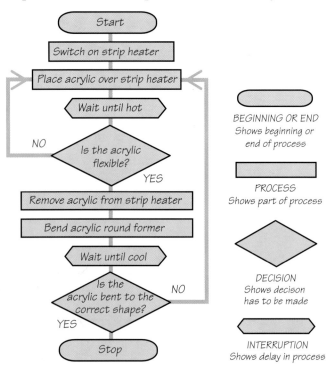

Fig. 1.69 *A flow chart showing the stages in bending a piece of acrylic.*

Fig. 1.70

Block diagrams

Action planning requires you to be logical, as you must work out exactly what needs to be done and in what order. The simplest way to plan is to make a **block diagram**. To do this, write down all the tasks in the correct order. Then draw a box around each task (you may be able to group related tasks together in one box). The boxes show the stages of the making process. Link the boxes together with arrows to show the order of the stages. A block diagram of a system is shown on page 1.8 (Fig 1.44).

Flow charts

The stages involved in making something can be shown on a flow chart like the one shown in Fig. 1.69. A number of different symbols are used to show the various types of action involved in the making process. The British Standards Institution has recommended a list of symbols so that everyone can recognise them. They are shown in Fig. 1.70.

Making

After you have planned your D&T project work you are ready to turn your ideas into reality (realisation). This is the making stage. For many people, this is the most enjoyable and exciting part of D&T.

Be prepared ➡

In most cases making your product will not be too difficult. If you have thought carefully about what you are going to make, and planned and prepared properly, then the making should be very straightforward.

Fig. 1.71 *If you have planned carefully, the making of your product should not be difficult*

⬅ Ask for help and advice

You may need to ask for help with techniques and materials that are new to you. Your teacher will be available for help so don't forget to ask. Sometimes they may not know all the answers themselves and they may send you to an expert. Remember that your teachers have different specialist skills. Many are experts in a particular area and it is important for you to use their strengths where you can.

Fig. 1.72 *Don't be reluctant to ask for help and advice*

Aim for quality ➡

Always aim to produce work of the highest quality. Remember, what you make might last a long time. Be as accurate as you can when working with materials and present your work as neatly as you can. Select and match materials that will help you to create a quality piece of work. If you are not happy with your skill in a particular technique, practise it before using it in your project work.

Fig. 1.73 *Always work safely*

 ## Work Safely

Safety is very important when working with tools, materials and equipment, as it is at this stage when accidents are most likely to happen. Always try to be aware of the dangers when using practical areas, and work as safely as possible. Keep the area around you clean and tidy, and put things away when you have finished with them. Never run in workshops or practical rooms, and always take great care when handling sharp tools or hot materials. Protect yourself by wearing suitable protective clothing, and always follow safety precautions.

Think about the accidents that could occur when you are working in practical areas. Make a list of what you could do to prevent these accidents from happening.

Evaluation and testing

Evaluating is a natural part of designing for most people. It is very unusual for a person to make something without considering how successful it is, or how difficult it was to produce. Only a few people are completely satisfied with their work. Most people, if they are being honest with themselves, will be able to suggest improvements that they could make. You may even evaluate your work without realising it – when you reject some of your first ideas, for example. This will certainly happen as you become more experienced in designing and making.

Fig. 1.74 *A cyclist's helmet being evaluated by impact testing against a simulated kerb stone*

Evaluating is very important in business and in industry. Companies evaluate how they make things so that they produce goods as efficiently as possible. Consumers are sometimes asked to evaluate products and services so that companies can find out the consumers' needs. Many products that appear to be new on the market are the result of industrial designers redesigning and changing existing ones.

Evaluation as a starting point

In school you may be asked to evaluate existing products and then improve or redesign them. This is using evaluating as a starting point.

Evaluating your finished product →

To evaluate your finished product you need to have something to judge it against. If you have no comparison for your product your evaluation will consist of general statements that are vague and meaningless. Think back to the specification. Do you remember how you thought carefully about the criteria that the finished product must satisfy? You can now evaluate your finished product against those original criteria. Does it fulfil all the criteria in the specification or just some of them?

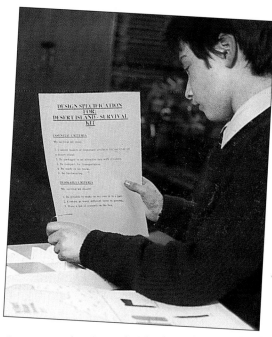

Fig. 1.75 *Evaluating a finished product in school*

Checklist

1. What were my original aims?

2. How does my finished product meet these aims?

3. How successful is the product? Does it work?

4. Am I happy with the results?

5. What do other people think about my design work?

6. Can I improve the product in any way?

Fig. 1.76 *Evaluation checklist*

Other people's evaluation

You must always try to be objective when evaluating your own work. Sometimes it is easier to evaluate other people's work. Why not ask someone else to evaluate your finished product for you? Record their views and use the information in your final evaluation. You might decide to carry out a survey and see what several different people think about your design work.

Improving your finished product

Could you improve your finished product in any way? You are either very lucky, or a very talented designer, if the answer to that question is no. Nearly every piece of work can be improved. It may be something simple such as changing the colour of the product, or it may be much more complicated and involve improving the product's performance. You may be given the opportunity not only to suggest improvements, but to carry them out. This will depend on how much time is available for the project. It is a good idea to leave some time at the end of a project to make improvements to your product.

Fig. 1.77 *Pupils testing the strength of a paper tube*

As part of your evaluation you will need to test your design. Testing can cover a variety of activities. Materials can be tested to see if they are suitable to use for a particular task. Finished products can be tested to see if they work successfully.

Testing and choosing materials

By testing materials you can find out more about their properties. For example, you may want to compare different materials to find out which is stronger, lighter or more hardwearing. These tests are known as comparative tests and the results will help you to decide which is the most suitable material to use for a particular design. Find out if there is any equipment in your school that can be used to test materials. It is possible to design and make simple test equipment yourself (Fig. 1.77).

User testing

It is a good idea to let the people who are going to use your product test it for you. For example, if you have designed and made a toy or a game, why not let children test it and give you their reactions (see Fig. 1.78)?

(N.B. First, make sure your product is safe.)

User testing is often carried out in industry before a new product is launched. Groups of potential users are asked for their reactions and opinions about a new product.

Fig. 1.78 *Children testing a toy*

Product testing

Perhaps the best way to evaluate the success of your final product is to use it for what it is intended. Don't forget to keep a record of what happens during testing. It might be necessary for you to change or improve your product after it has been thoroughly tested. In industry, once the design work is complete, a limited number of products are produced for testing and evaluating. These are called prototypes and are designed to be tested so that any faults or problems can be found before large numbers of the product are manufactured. Prototypes are often tested to see if they are hardwearing. For example, washing machine prototypes are tested to see if they will continue working properly for many years. Designers learn a great deal from the results of these tests and use the information to improve their products.

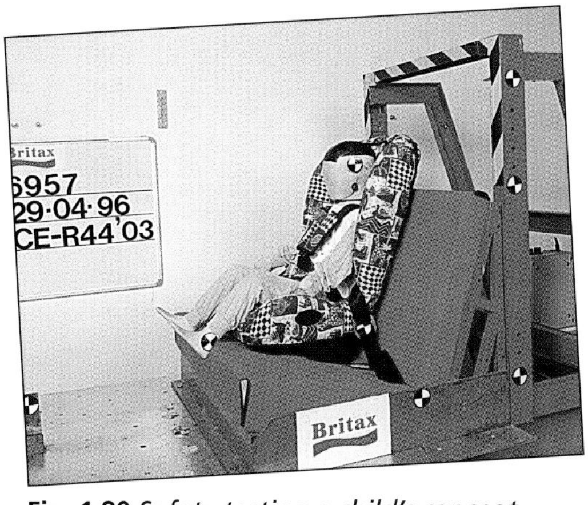

Fig. 1.79 *Polymer testing at an IBM factory*

Safety testing

As a designer you have a responsibility to the people who will use your products and to the environment. It is very important that what you design and make is safe to use and will not harm anyone. There are very strict rules and regulations which manufacturers in this country must keep. These are known as British Standards, and many products are stamped with the British Standard number that applies to them. For example, a 13-amp plug must be made so that it conforms to British Standard 1363A. Make sure that your products are as safe as possible, especially if they are to be used by young children.

Fig. 1.80 *Safety testing a child's car seat*

Using IT

Information Technology can be a very useful and versatile tool in D&T. It will help you to investigate and gather information, and organise the information once you have gathered it. It can be used to help you present your design proposals as well as make working drawings. It can even help you to make the product itself.

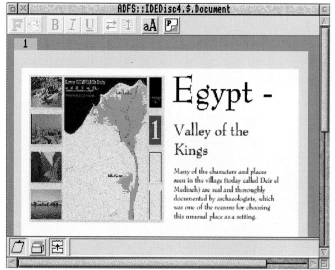

Fig. 1.81

Desk top publishing

Desk top publishing (DTP) software allows you to include graphics, drawings and, in some cases, photographs with your text (Fig. 1.81). You can make the drawings yourself using a graphics program or you can use drawings that are already available on a disk. There are collections of drawings, called 'clip art', available on disk for use in a computer.

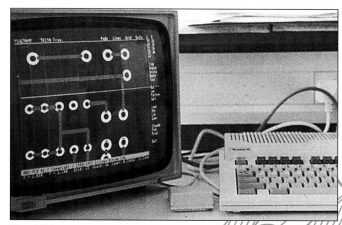

Fig. 1.82

Computer-aided design →

Designing on a computer screen is known as computer aided design (CAD). It is an example of two-dimensional modelling. It is possible to use the computer in a variety of ways – from simple drawing programs to complicated CAD systems. Fig. 1.82 shows an electronic circuit that has been modelled using a computer software package. Fig. 1.83 shows how a fitted bedroom has been designed on a computer and the design printed out for the customer. It is possible to design like this yourself using a computer software package, such as TechSoft Designer.

Fig. **1.84** *Designs produced with TechSoft Designer*

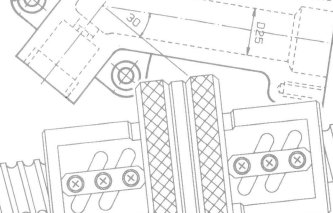

Fig. 1.83

Computer-aided manufacture

Computers can be used to control the machines that manufacture the product. They have been used to do this in industry for many years. This process is known as computer-aided manufacture (CAM).

CAD/CAM ➡

When computer-aided design work is produced by computer-controlled machines, the process is called CAD/CAM. The Roland CAMM–1 desktop sign maker (see Fig. 1.85) allows CAD/CAM to be carried out very simply in schools. A design drawn on a CAD system can be printed out using a pen on paper, or it can be cut out of card or coloured vinyl by using a carbide-tipped cutter. This provides an excellent way of making cardboard models and signs.

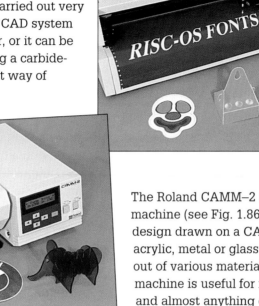

Fig. 1.85

The Roland CAMM–2 computer-aided engraving machine (see Fig. 1.86) works in a similar way. A design drawn on a CAD system can be engraved on acrylic, metal or glass. The design can also be cut out of various materials very accurately. The machine is useful for making jewellery, acrylic signs and almost anything else that requires very accurate cutting out.

Fig. 1.86

⬅ Computer numerical control

The engineering industry uses a type of computer-aided manufacture known as computer numerical control (CNC). Programs made up of a series of numbers are used to control and operate the machines. It may be possible for you to use CNC in your work. Computer programs such as TechSoft CNC Designer allow you to design an object on the screen and then make it using computer-controlled machines. Fig. 1.87 shows the stages involved in making a product using CAD/CAM and CNC lathe.

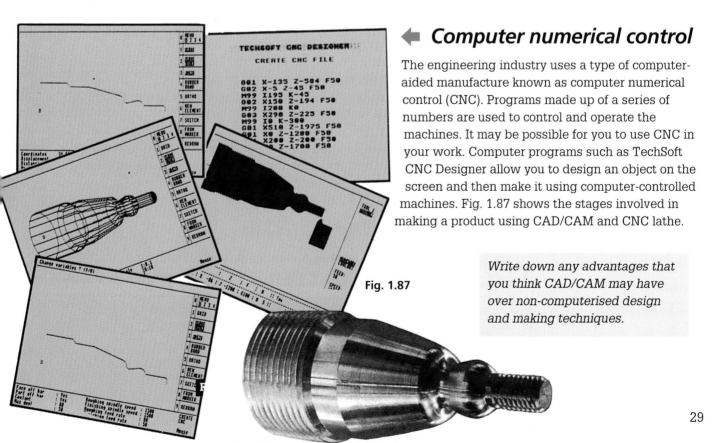

Fig. 1.87

Write down any advantages that you think CAD/CAM may have over non-computerised design and making techniques.

2 MATERIALS

Every day we come into contact with many different materials. Everything constructed by people is made from some type of material.

The development of humans and the materials that they use are closely linked. Historians have named periods of history after the most important material used by people at that time: for example, the Stone Age, the Bronze Age and the Iron Age.

Fig. 2.1 *Stone Age implements*

Ever since people started to make things they have had problems finding the best materials for the job. Even when they found the right material they had to find a way of shaping it. To shape it they needed other materials which were harder or tougher than the first material.

To begin with, the obvious materials to use were those readily available, such as wood, stone, clay, bones, animal skins and plants. These were used to make weapons, tools and clothes. Gradually, over thousands of years, new materials were discovered and tried out, like bronze, iron, glass and precious metals. Each new material offered new possibilities. Metals were an especially important step forward, because of their strength and the simple ways in which they could be shaped to make tools, weapons and even jewellery.

The materials that have had the most impact in the 20th century are concrete and plastics. Concrete has influenced our buildings and plastics have become such a part of our lives that we would find it difficult to imagine life without them. Every day it seems that new uses are found for plastics. You use them to comb your hair, brush your teeth, pack your lunch in and to carry your shopping. Plastics are also used for underground water pipes and parts of cars. There is even research going on into developing a plastic car engine.

Fig. 2.3 *Plastics in use*

Fig. 2.2 *Manufacturing*

Classifying materials

Materials can be classified (arranged) into two groups. A material is either natural or manufactured (made by people).

Natural		**Manufactured**	
	wood		plastic
	clay		metal
	leather		paper
	stone		brick
			card

Choosing Materials

It is important to choose the right materials for each thing that you design. If you choose the wrong materials, it may break, corrode, or not work at all. In order to make the right choices, you need to understand what each material can do, what it is good for and what its limitations are. For example, plastics are very good insulators, but often they cannot be used where there is a lot of heat. These properties make plastic a good material for a saucepan handle, but less satisfactory for the body of the saucepan (Fig. 2.5).

Fig 2.5

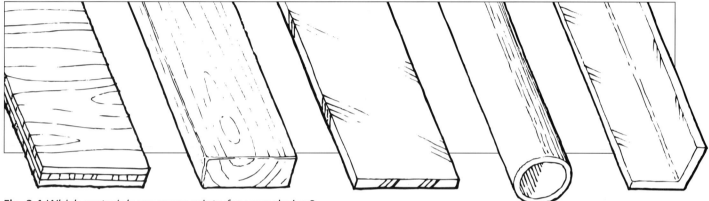

Fig. 2.4 *Which materials are appropriate for your design?*

Fig 2.6 *What properties does your material need to have?*

Why are plastics used for so many things?
Make a list of the properties that the materials used to build an airplane would need.

How to choose

When choosing a material for a project you must ask yourself;

What properties does the material need to have?
How strong does it need to be?
Does it need to be rigid or flexible?
Should it be light or heavy?
Does it need to be weatherproof?
Is colour important?
What kind of finish will it have?

Only by asking questions like these can you make the right choice of material. Even then, there are still some things you need to find out.

Is the material you want available?
What will it cost?
How will you shape and join it?

It is no good choosing a material if you cannot get it or it is too expensive.

You might decide gold would be the ideal material for a piece of jewellery, but it is unlikely that you could afford to use it.

Only by finding the answers to all these questions can you find the right material for the job. This chapter aims to give you the information needed to help you choose the right materials when you are making design decisions.

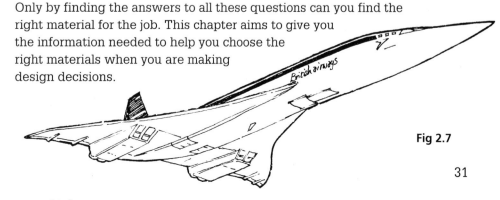

Fig 2.7

Materials: Wood

Wood is a natural material that has been used for many centuries by builders and craftspeople. Until recently it has been easily available and there has been a seemingly endless supply. However, it takes trees at least 30 years (and some over 100 years) to mature and produce wood suitable for human use. If trees are cut down at a faster rate than they are planted, soon there will be little wood to use. The clearing of rain forests is an example of this kind of destruction.

There are two basic types of wood: **hardwood** and **softwood**. Hardwoods are generally harder than softwoods and come from broad-leafed deciduous trees (which lose their leaves in autumn), like oak, elm and beech. Softwoods come from conifers – evergreen trees which keep their needles all year round. They are not usually as heavy as hardwoods.

Fig. 2.8 *Broad leafed hardwood tree*

Fig. 2.9 *Needle covered softwood tree*

Growth ➡

The energy in sunlight is combined with water, minerals and carbon dioxide by the trees to provide them with the food they need to grow. Each year a new layer of growth is added just below the bark, producing an **annual ring**. You can tell a tree's age by the number of annual rings it has. New growth is called **sapwood**. Over a period of years,new layers grow on the outside and the centre hardens to form **heartwood**.

Heartwood, therefore, is found at the centre of a tree, surrounded by the new layers of sapwood and the bark. The heartwood is the best part of a tree to use for manufacturing, because of its hardness and strength.

Trees grow by producing cells which are long and thin. These become the 'wood'. We call the pattern of the cells the **grain**. It is the grain that gives the different types of wood their distinctive appearance. Look at Fig. 2.11. The magnified views show the grain in detail.

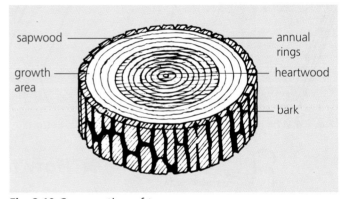

Fig. 2.10 *Cross section of tree*

The grain

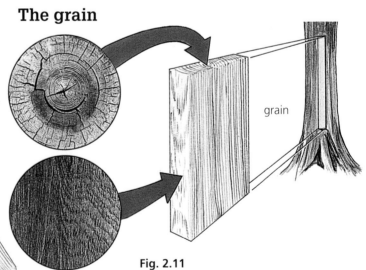

Fig. 2.11

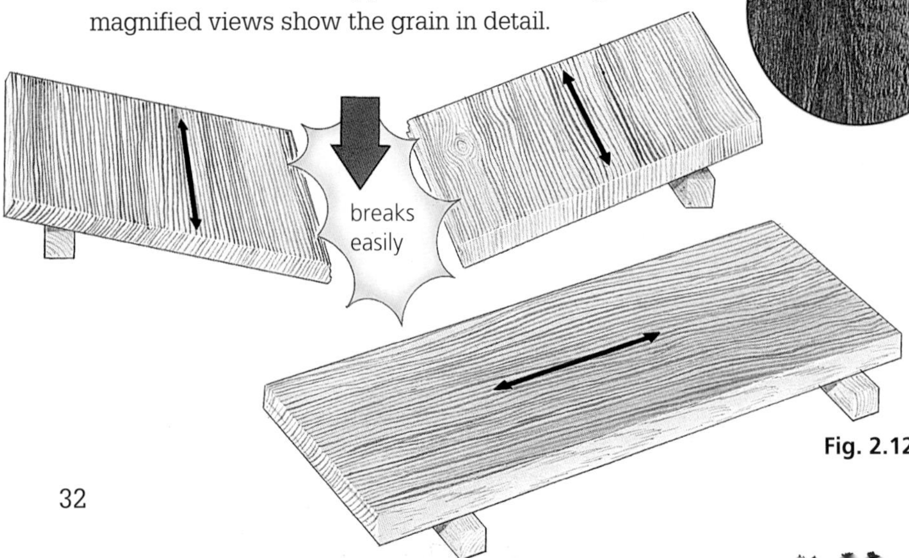

Fig. 2.12

The way that the grain is fastened together gives a clue to the fact that wood is stronger in one direction than the other. This is important. Wood is always cut with the grain in the long direction of the plank (see Fig. 2.12).

Preparing for use

When a tree is initially cut into planks, they contain a lot of water. If they were used in this state they would shrink, split and twist. The water content is reduced to about 10% by a process called **seasoning**. This can be done over a few days using a special kiln or over several years by leaving the wood stacked neatly in the open air.

Softwoods

Softwoods are softer, easier to cut and not as hardwearing as hardwoods. They grow faster and are usually lighter in colour. The **grain** is very easy to see, showing as dark lines on a pale background.

Softwoods are cheaper than hardwoods. They are used a lot in the building industry for roofs and window frames. Softwood is know as 'pine' or 'deal', making no distinction between the different types. Two examples of softwoods are Redwood and Parana pine.

Redwood is honey coloured, with very definite grain lines and knots. It is usually straight grained and easy to cut with saws and planes. It is used a lot for house roofs, window frames and skirting boards.

Parana pine is a pale yellow colour with attractive reddish brown streaks. It is often used for good-quality joinery, such as staircases.

Fig. 2.13 *Roof timbers made from softwood*

1. *Why are internal door frames made from softwood?*
2. *What do you think would happen if a builder used chipboard to make the roof of a house?*

Hardwoods

Hardwoods are harder and heavier than softwoods. They come in many different colours. Hardwoods are generally used for high-quality work, such as furniture. Mahogany and beech are two of the more common hardwoods.

Mahogany is reddish brown in colour and is both hard and strong. It is often used for top-quality furniture.

Beech is pinkish brown in colour with small gold flecks. It is very hard and strong. It is used for mallets, workbenches and wooden kitchen tools. It is also used a lot for school furniture.

Fig. 2.14 *Products made from hardwoods*

Manufactured Boards

Manufactured Boards are made by cutting up solid timber and sticking it back together again in a different way. This is a good way of making large boards which stay flat. Large boards cut directly from a tree trunk are quite strong but they can warp.

Medium density fibre board (MDF) is made by gluing and compressing together thousands of tiny wood particles to form a dense, solid board. Kitchen units, decorative mouldings and items of furniture are made from MDF which is covered in a thin layer of wood or plastic.

Plywood is made by sticking together thin layers of wood called **veneers**. Each layer has its grain in the opposite direction to the ones next to it. This keeps the boards flat and makes them very strong. It is used for things like drawer bottoms, toys and interior doors. It is often very thin.

Blockboard is made by gluing strips of softwood side by side, and then sticking a thin veneer on each side. It is made in thicknesses of 12 mm upwards and is very strong. Blockboard is often used for making modern furniture.

Chipboard is made by gluing and compressing together thousands of tiny bits of wood. It is not very strong and is difficult to join. However, it is cheap. It is often used with a facing veneer for modern furniture, such as kitchen cupboards.

Hardboard is made by gluing and compressing pulped wood. One side is rough and the other smooth. It comes in thin sheets and is used to cover large areas cheaply, such as cupboard backs. It is not very strong.

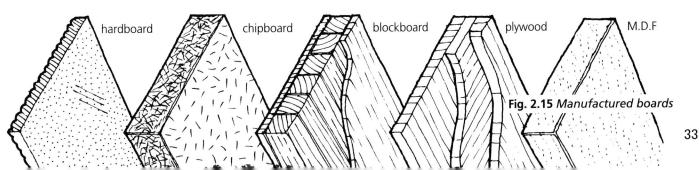

Fig. 2.15 *Manufactured boards*

33

Materials: Metal

Metal is a very important material. It was first used to make tools and weapons thousands of years ago. Rare and precious metals were once used as currency; nowadays inexpensive metal and paper money is used instead. Metal has enabled inventors and designers to produce many useful things over the centuries – ploughs, clocks, steam engines, sewing machines and motor vehicles – all of which could not be made without metal.

Fig. 2.16 *Iron bridge built in 1779*

Fig. 2.17 *Bronze Age axe and shield*   **Fig. 2.18** *Medieval armour*

Fig. 2.19 *Brunel's iron clad ship the Great Britain*

Metal is found in the earth's surface. It is rarely found as pure metal but usually in the form of ore where it is combined with chemicals and other materials such as rock and earth. There are two basic types of metal: **ferrous** and **non-ferrous**. Ferrous metal contains iron, and non-ferrous metal contains no iron. Before it can be used the metal must be removed from the ore. Some metals are removed by a process of heating known as smelting while others are removed chemically.

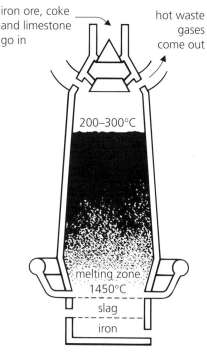

iron ore, coke and limestone go in

hot waste gases come out

200–300°C

melting zone 1450°C

slag

iron

Fig. 2.20 *A blast furnace*

Iron is removed from iron ore in a blast furnace where it is mixed with coke and limestone and heated until the metal melts. Aluminium, a non-ferrous metal, is found in the form of clay like material called bauxite. Alumina is removed from the bauxite chemically and made into aluminium by an electrolytic process.

Fig. 2.21 *An iron works*

Fig. 2.22 *Metal shapes*

When metals are melted they can be poured into shaped moulds. This is called casting and is used to make products such as a vice. Metals are very versatile materials. They can be stamped with a pattern, as with coins, made into thin sheets, pressed and painted, as with a car body. Metals can be joined and sealed as in containers for food and drinks. They can be very strong yet light, as in aircraft, or used for delicate decoration as, for example, when making jewellery. Metals can also conduct electricity and heat.

Ferrous metals and alloys

The primary constituent of ferrous alloys is iron. Ferrous materials have the disadvantage that they become rusty. The only way to stop the rusting is to put a protective layer on the surface of the metal, such as paint or enamel. Despite this protection, many ferrous metal products still end up rusty and rotten.

Tool steel

This contains about 1% carbon. It is used to make tools, such as screwdrivers and hammers (Fig.2.23), because it can be hardened, making it strong enough for the job.

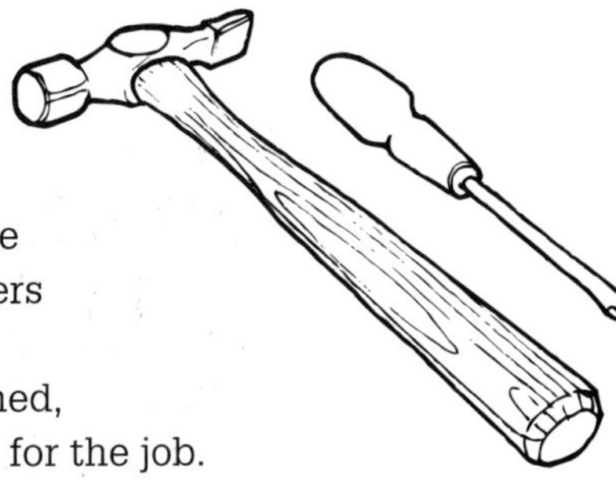

Mild steel

This is one of the most common ferrous metals and the softest one. It is grey in colour. It contains about 0.3% carbon. It is used for nuts and bolts, stool legs and car bodies. It is the cheapest metal and so is used a lot in D&T.

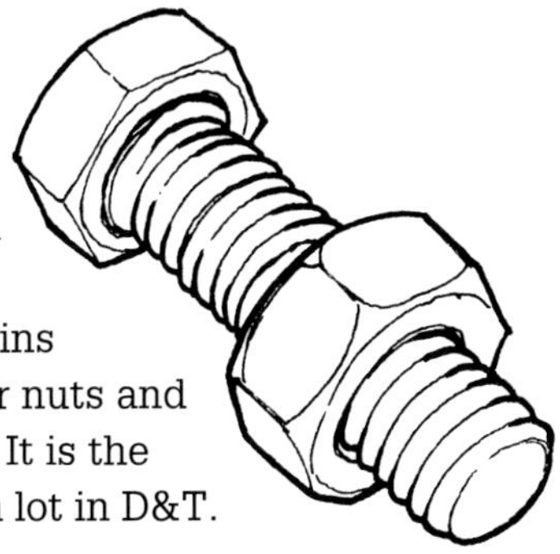

Fig. 2.23

Fig. 2.24 *Mild steel is used for nuts and bolts*

Cast Iron

This is heavy, hard and brittle. It is used for vices, such as that in Fig. 2.25, drill stands and car engines. These shapes can only be made by casting. It is used very little in D&T.

Stainless Steel

Many new metal alloys have been created, which have extra hardness, extra strength or extra resistance to corrosion. For example, stainless steel has been developed, which does not go rusty in water like other steel.

Tin Plate

This is mild steel with a very thin layer of tin on the surface to stop it rusting. It scratches very easily. It is used for tin cans (Fig.2.27).

Fig. 2.25 *Vice*

Fig. 2.26 *Stainless steel cutlery*

Fig. 2.27 *Tin can*

Non-Ferrous metals and alloys

These are metals and alloys which do not contain iron and therefore do not go rusty. This makes them very useful for jobs where they may come into contact with moisture. It also means that they do not need a protective coating. You will have seen many items made of non-ferrous metals. They are usually bright and shiny if kept clean. If left they go dull.

The dull layer on the surface does not hurt the metal, in fact it protects it. Many non-ferrous metals are expensive, such as gold, silver and platinum. It is not surprising that they are not normally used in schools! Even the most common ones are more expensive than most ferrous metals.

Copper

This is quite tough, but easily shaped and pinkish brown in colour. It conducts heat and electricity well and can be shaped and soldered easily, but it is quite expensive. It is used for water pipes, cisterns and electrical wires. It is often used in the form of sheets and tubes.

Aluminium

This is light, soft, easily shaped and silvery grey in colour. It conducts heat and electricity well. It is used to make window frames, saucepans, cooking foil and aircraft. It is used a lot in D&T because it is easy to work and can be polished to give a smooth finish.

Fig. 2.29 *Aluminium saucepan*

Brass

This is an alloy of copper and zinc. It is heavy, quite hard and gold in colour. It is similar to copper in many ways, but with greater strength.

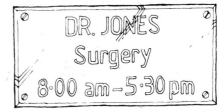

Fig. 2.30 *Brass nameplate*

Fig. 2.28 *Copper pipe*

1. *Why do we need to use special steel for cutlery?*
2. *How is aluminum produced?*

Materials: Plastics

Plastics were once made from natural things such as plants, insects and animal products. Nowadays, however, most of the plastics we use are made from refined crude oil

The word plastic means easily shaped. There are several different kinds of plastic. Their correct names are not easy to remember, for example, polyvynilchloride, polypropylene and polymethylmethacrylate. However, many of these plastics are known by names which are much easier to remember, for example, polyvynilchloride is more commonly known as PVC.

Plastics can be made to have almost any property that is required. They can be soft or hard, light or heavy, strong or weak. They are made by a chemical 'cooking' process. The ingredients are simple, but the number of different outcomes is almost limitless.

There are two families of plastics – thermosetting plastics (including resins) and thermoplastics.

Fig. 2.31 *Oil rig*

Thermosetting plastic

Thermosetting plastics will melt the first time they are heated. However when cooled the plastic sets. The polymers that make up the plastic bond permanently together and it remains hard even if it is reheated.

Thermosetting plastics are usually made into products by heating powder in a mould. They are used to make such things as electric plugs and sockets, light switches and kitchen spoons. These plastics are not often used in school D&T.

Phenol formaldehyde

This is dark, hard and quite brittle. It is used for saucepan handles and cheap electrical fittings.

Fig. 2.32 *Saucepan handle*

Polyester Resin

This comes as a thick liquid which can be used in two ways. The clear version of this resin is used for 'casting' (embedding), as when making a paperweight. The 'lay up' version of this resin is used along with sheets of glass fibre to make glass reinforced plastic (GRP) mouldings, (e.g. for motorbike top boxes, boat hulls or some car bodies).

Fig. 2.33 *Paperweight made from polyester resin*

Epoxy Resin

This is used to make glues, such as 'Araldite' (which sticks most things) and 'Aerolite' (a waterproof wood glue).

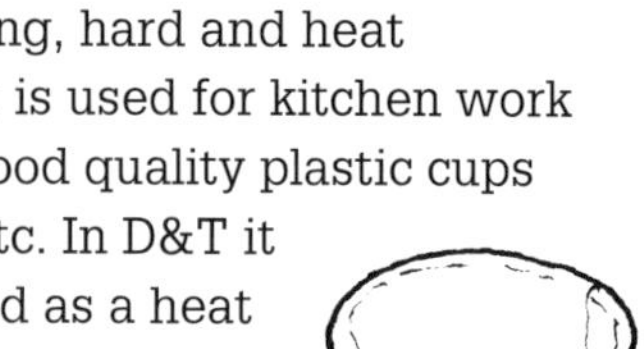

Fig. 2.34 *Araldite: adhesive and hardener*

Melamine formaldehyde

This is strong, hard and heat resistant. It is used for kitchen work surfaces, good quality plastic cups (Fig 2.35) etc. In D&T it may be used as a heat resistant or decorative surface finish.

Fig. 2.35 *Plastic mug*

Urea formaldehyde

This is usually white in colour, tough and attractive to look at. It is used for good quality electrical fittings, such as plugs, light switches, etc.

Fig. 2.36 *Light switch*

Thermoplastics

Thermoplastics can be softened by heating, even when they have been heated before – they will always set again when cooled. This allows the plastic to be bent, twisted and stretched easily. If heated further, thermoplastics can be squeezed out into shapes, like squeezing toothpaste out of a tube. This process is called extrusion. They can also be shaped by heating and then blown, like bubble gum, into shaped holes to produce bottles. Thermoplastics are good insulators of electricity, so they can be used to coat electrical cables.

Fig. 2.37 *Acrylic is used for shops signs*

Acrylic

Acrylic is the most common plastic used in school D&T. Its chemical name is polymethylmethacrylate but most people just call it acrylic. It is available in many different colours as sheets or as round rods. Acrylic is an attractive material and it can resist the weather very well. These properties make it ideal for signs outside shops (see Fig. 2.37).

Acrylic can be softened and bent, blown or twisted to many different shapes. When clear, it can be used as windows and is much stronger than glass, although it will scratch fairly easily. It is used in aircraft windows because it is so tough.

Fig. 2.38 *Electronic computer games housed in acrylic*

Rigid polystyrene

This is used for containers such as cosmetic bottles and TV cabinets. In its sheet form it is used to make disposable cups. It is used in D&T to make simple shapes by vacuum forming (see Forming Plastics on page 50).

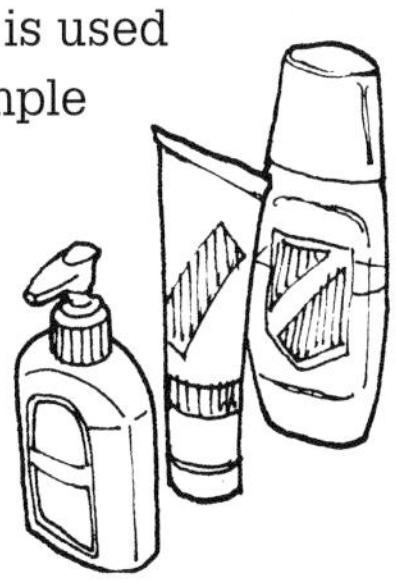

Fig. 2.39 *Cosmetic bottles*

High density polythene

This is strong and stiff. It is used for washing-up bowls, buckets and bleach bottles.

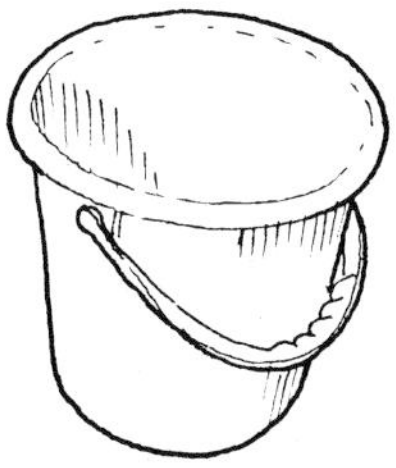

Fig. 2.40 *Plastic bucket*

Low density polystyrene

This is tough and flexible. It is used for washing-up liquid bottles, transparent packaging and plastic bags. It is used in D&T for vacuum forming.

Fig. 2.41 *Washing up liquid bottle*

Expanded polystyrene

This is used as white granular packaging to prevent damage to fragile goods in transit. It can be used in D&T to make moulds for lost polystyrene casting (see Casting on page 53).

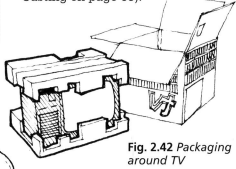

Fig. 2.42 *Packaging around TV*

Rigid PVC

This is used for drain pipes and guttering (Fig. 2.43).

Fig. 2.43

Flexible PVC

This is used for inflatable dinghies, hose pipes, shoes and upholstery material.

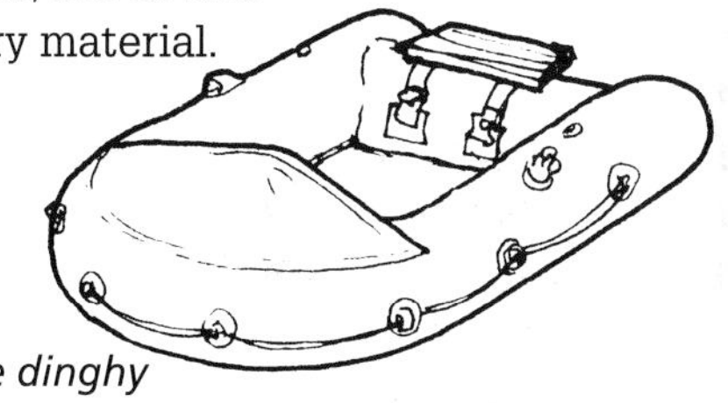

Fig. 2.44 *Inflatable dinghy*

Re-cycling plastics

The use of plastics for containers, from plastic bags to shaped chocolate boxes, has become very common today. Plastics do create problems, however. They don't rot very easily – they are **non bio-degradable**. Some plastics can be recycled and used again. As most plastics are made from oil, which is a non-renewable resource, recycling is becoming increasingly necessary.

1. *Does plastic have any disadvantages in everyday use?*
2. *What is the main difference between thermosetting plastics and thermoplastics?*
3. *Make a list of things that are made from acrylic.*

3 WORKING WITH MATERIALS

Manufactured products have to be made to the highest possible standards and be as cost effective as possible. To achieve this, designers have to take into account the properties of the materials they are going to use and the best way of harnessing the strengths of those materials in the manufacturing process. This chapter will show you the basic forming processes that are used in manufacturing, and that you will use in school – wasting, reforming, deforming and fabrication.

Wasting

This is the process of removing material. Examples include sawing, filing, planing, lathe work, carving, drilling and machining.

Reforming

This involves changing the material by melting or chemical mixing. Casting (melting and re-setting metal in a shaped mould) is one example. Casting plastic materials, for example by injection moulding using semi liquids is a further example of a reforming technique.

Fig. 3.1 *Working with wood*

Deforming

This involves the changing of the shape of the material without wasting. Examples of this include forging, beaten metal work, laminating wood, bending and vacuum forming plastics.

Fig. 3.2 *Fabricating using wood*

This chapter will look at both hand crafts and machine processes. Although you will be working with different materials, many of the techniques will be the same – marking out, measuring and using holding devices. The most important common factor is **safety**, this must be considered first.

Fabrication

This is the process of joining materials together. Most constructional products will require some fabrication in their manufacture. Examples of fabrication methods include wood joints, screws, rivets, welding, brazing, soldering and gluing.

Fig. 3.3 *Working with plastic*

Fig. 3.4 *Deforming hot metal*

Fig. 3.5

CHECK OUT THIS DUDE, HE AIN'T SO COOL – HOW MANY WAYS DOES HE BREAK THE RULE?

> ⚠️ # Work safely
>
> When you are making your design it is most important to make it safely, using safe working practices in a safe working environment. The single most common cause of accidents in the workshops is human carelessness. To create a safe working environment you will need to work in a mature and sensible manner. Always follow instructions and safety rules carefully.

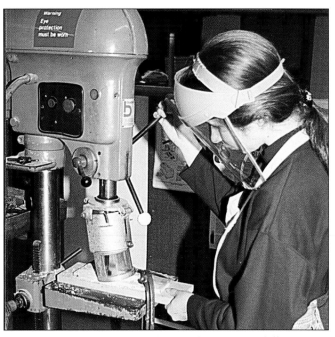

Fig. 3.6 *Always use protective equipment, especially eye protection*

How you dress

■ Before starting work with tools and equipment, especially machines, remove or tuck in ties, take off jewellery and tie back long hair.

■ Wear aprons or overalls to protect clothes, and stout shoes.

■ Wear special protective clothing and eye protection when required.

How you behave

■ Behave sensibly at all times.

■ Move around with care and carry tools sensibly.

■ Report immediately any accident or breakage.

■ You are responsible for your friends' safety. Be vigilant when you and they are using tools.

HIGHLY FLAMMABLE

Wash hands

Danger Solvents

Fig. 3.7 *Be aware of safety symbols*

Safe working practice

■ Keep your work area clean and tidy.

■ Check the condition of tools and report any which are blunt or broken.

■ When using sharp edged tools remember to keep both hands behind the blade.

■ Clean equipment and the work area after use.

■ Report faults and problems.

A safe working environment

■ Leave hot tools and metals in a safe place to cool. Inform others by using a HOT sign.

■ Always read the instructions on chemicals, glues, solvents etc.

■ Consult your teacher about the disposal of any chemical waste, including paper towels and cloths.

■ Avoid inhaling large amounts of dust – wear a face mask when using power sanders.

■ Clean and wash hands thoroughly after work.

Draw a sketch map of your D&T room and mark on it the following: emergency exits; gangways to emergency exits that must be kept as 'clearways'; fire extinguishers and what type of fire they are for; emergency stop buttons; first aid boxes (state who you should tell if someone hurts themselves); and the place you should assemble if there is a fire.

Marking out

When materials are to be cut to shape or formed they should be marked out first. This means that lines are placed on the surface of the material to show where the cuts or bends are to be made.

The different surfaces of metal, wood, card and plastic require different marking tools.

Making the marks

Paper and card

A pencil is the best tool to use on paper and card. A pencil with a soft lead ('B' pencil) allows you to correct your mistakes by rubbing out your lines. A hard pencil ('H' pencil) produces a crisp, thin line but will not be as easy to rub out.

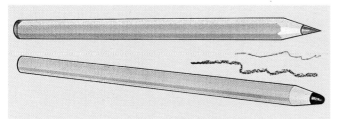

Fig. 3.8 *A hard pencil and a soft pencil*

Plastic

Plastic requires a spirit-based marker pen. These pens come in different thicknesses. You should use a thin one for greatest accuracy. The lines can be removed by cleaning the plastic with solvent. You could also use a chinagraph pencil to mark out plastic.

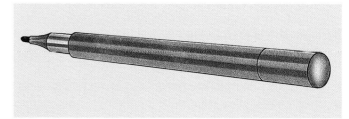

Fig. 3.10 *Marker pen*

Wood

When marking out wood you can use a pencil or a marking knife. With a pencil you can draw curved shapes using a pair of compasses or draw around a template. With a marking knife you can make a clear, thin cut across the grain.

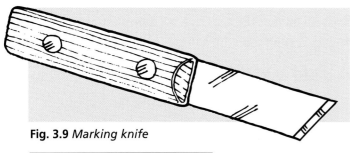

Fig. 3.9 *Marking knife*

Metal

Marks are usually made on metal with a scriber. If the metal is first coated with marking blue (a blue die), the marks show up much better. A spirit-based marker pen is often used on sheet aluminium. Deep marks must be polished away.

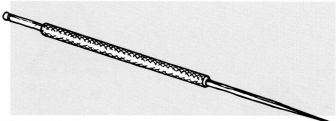

Fig. 3.11 *Scriber*

Holes

Before you drill a hole you need to mark its centre. Before drilling metal you must make a small dent to stop the drill slipping. To do this you need to use a centre punch and a hammer see Fig. 3.12. If the hole is an unusual shape, like those shown in Fig. 3.13, you will have to mark its outline. Most of the waste can then be removed by drilling. The remainder can be removed by filing.

Fig. 3.12 *Using a centre punch*

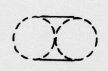

Fig. 3.13

Guiding the marks

To produce straight, curved or odd-shaped lines you may need special tools to guide the pen, pencil or other marking tool.

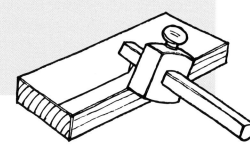

Fig. 3.14 *A marking gauge*

Straight lines ➡

To draw straight lines you will need to use different tools to guide you. For lines parallel to an edge you should use either a marking gauge for wood (see Fig. 3.14) or a pair of odd-leg calipers for metal (see Fig. 3.15). Lines at right angles to an edge can be easily drawn using a try square (see Fig. 3.16). A rule or straight edge can be used for other straight lines (see Fig. 3.17).

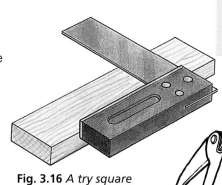

Fig. 3.16 *A try square*

Fig. 3.15 *Odd-leg calipers*

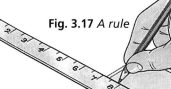

Fig. 3.17 *A rule*

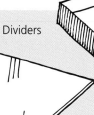
Compass   Dividers

◀ Curved lines

When drawing a circle or an arc (part of a circle) you will need to use of a pair of compasses for wood and plastic or a pair of dividers for metal (see Fig. 3.18).

Fig 3.18 *Compass and dividers*

Odd shapes ➡

To draw an odd shape, you can use a template to draw round (see Fig. 3.19). This also allows you to repeat the same shape as many times as you wish. Templates are used in industry where there are many repeated shapes to be cut out.

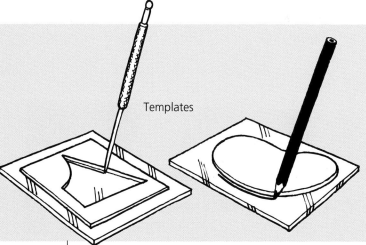
Templates

Fig. 3.19 *Using templates*

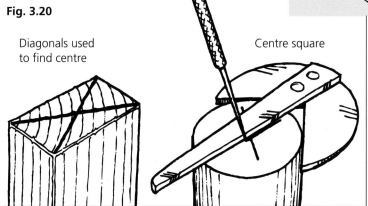

Fig. 3.20

Diagonals used to find centre   Centre square

◀ Finding centres

There will be times when you need to find the centre of a square, rectangular or round bar. A ruler and pencil can be used to draw the diagonals on the end of the square or rectangular pieces – the lines cross at the centre. For a round bar, use a centre square. Push it against the side of the bar and draw lines from two or three different positions (see Fig. 3.20). Where they cross is the centre.

Saws and sawing

Having marked out your material you will now need to shape it. Saws are used to remove large pieces of unwanted material quickly. There are many different types of saws, and you must be able to select from a few basic saws the one that will do the job required. This choice of tool is crucial if you are to work in a safe, efficient and accurate way.

Machine saws

Jigsaws are used to saw wood and plastic. They have a small blade that is moved up and down rapidly by an electric motor (see Fig. 3.21). The blade does not move far in either direction. The work to be cut is held firmly by hand on a flat cutting table. The work is then gently pressed against the moving blade. Curves can be cut by rotating the work as it reaches the blade. These saws, as with all machines in a workshop, should only be used with the permission of your teacher. If there is a guard fitted, it must be used.

Fig. 3.21 *A machine jigsaw*

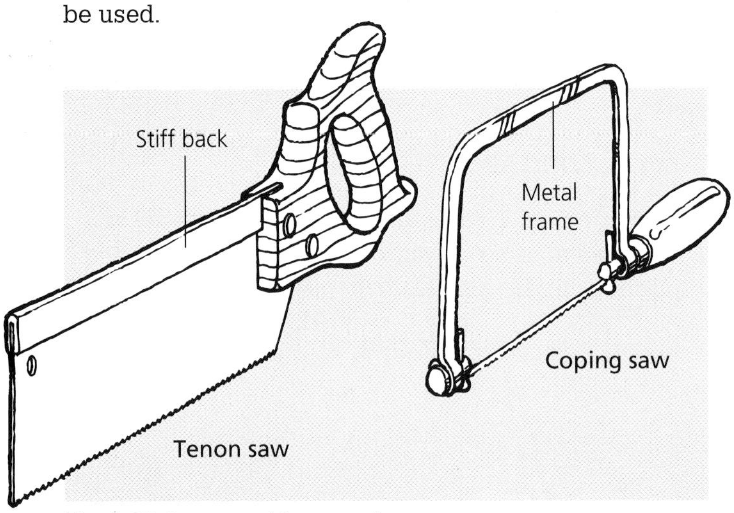

Fig. 3.22 *Saws used for wood*

Saws for wood

Tenon saws are used to cut pieces of wood to the right length. They are also used to saw straight lines when cutting joints. The wide blade does not allow you to cut curves. The blade is stiffened with a strip of metal along the top of the blade to stop it bending when you saw (see Fig. 3.22). You should always hold the wood being cut in a vice or use a bench hook (see Fig. 3.23).

Coping saws have thin blades, allowing you to make a curved cut. It is nearly impossible to cut a straight line with a coping saw, so use it only for curves. The blade is held in tension in a frame which allows you to twist the blade to cut in different directions (see Fig. 3.24).

Fig. 3.23 *Using a tenon saw and a bench hook to cut wood*

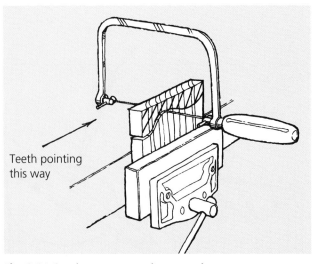

Fig. 3.24 *Sawing a curve using a coping saw*

Saws for metal

Hacksaws have replaceable blades that are held tightly in a frame (see Fig. 3.25). The blade is about 30 cm long and you can cut straight lines with it. When using a hacksaw, the teeth on the blade should point away from the handle to cut well.

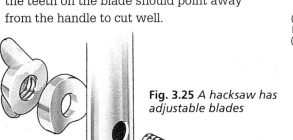

Fig. 3.25 *A hacksaw has adjustable blades*

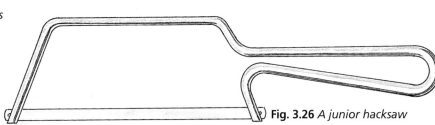

Fig. 3.26 *A junior hacksaw*

The junior hacksaw is a small version of the hacksaw with a shorter blade which has much smaller teeth (see Fig. 3.26). This saw is used to cut small, thin pieces of metal. Do not use it to cut thick pieces of metal – it will take far too long because the small teeth cut slowly, and the blade may break. Blades are also available for cutting wood.

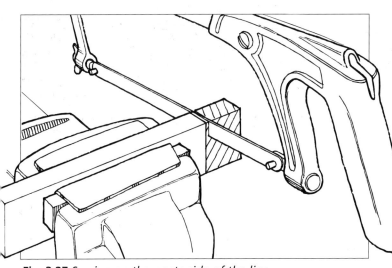

Fig. 3.27 *Sawing on the waste side of the line*

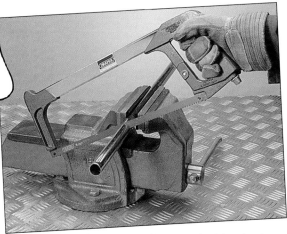

Fig. 3.28 *Cutting metal with a hacksaw*

Saws for acrylic

Jigsaws can be used to cut large sheets of acrylic. However, it is better to get your teacher to use the electrically-powered bandsaw to cut large sheets for you.

Coping saws are used to cut acrylic in the same way as they are used to saw wood. The sheet acrylic must be held securely in a vice close to the sawing point. If you allow the acrylic to flex whilst cutting it will probably break, so take care and cut gently. Work at a gentle, slowish pace because too much friction will cause heat that may melt the acrylic and result in the blade getting stuck.

Hacksaws are best used on metal (see above) but they can be used to cut acrylic. The only problem when using a hacksaw is that you must hold the acrylic very securely to prevent it from flexing and snapping.

⚠️ All saws cut wood. Fingers are softer than wood, metal or plastic so take great care when using any saw.

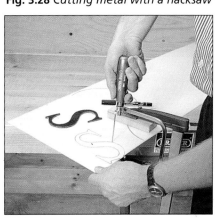

Fig. 3.29 *Using a coping saw to cut acrylic*

Making holes

You will need to produce many small holes when assembling pieces of wood, metal and plastic. They are all produced in a similar manner. A hand drill (wheelbrace) with twist drill can be used for small holes. Different twist drill bits produce different sized holes.

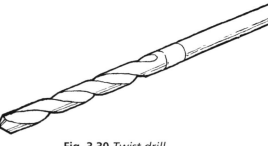

Fig. 3.30 *Twist drill*

Small holes

When making small holes you should use a vice or a clamp to make the material secure. To prevent thin acrylic sheets from splitting, a piece of scrap wood should be placed beneath your work.

Drilling by hand

To make correctly positioned and accurate holes you must take care. Hold the drill firmly and at right angles to your work. Press firmly but not too hard, and turn the handle slowly, speeding up when the hole is started.

Fig. 3.31 *A left-handed pupil using a hand drill*

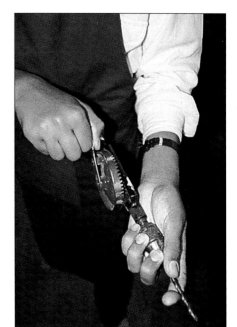

Fig. 3.32 *Changing the twist drill*

Large holes

A **carpenter's brace** is used to drill large holes in wood. Drill bits with tapered square shanks (ends) are used. The square shank makes it impossible for the bit to slip in the chuck during drilling. Drilling a hole without splitting the wood requires you to drill from both sides of the wood. First drill until the point shows on the other side of the wood (see Fig. 3.33), then turn it round and drill back into the hole using the small hole as a guide.

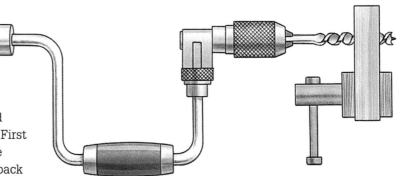

Fig. 3.33 *A carpenter's brace*

Fig. 3.34 *A drill bit*

A **forstner drill** bit is a special drill bit with a round shank that is used in the drilling machine (see Fig. 3.35). The work must be clamped to the drilling table very securely. These drills give smooth-sided, flat-bottomed holes in wood.

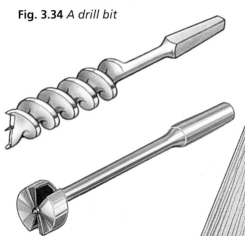

⬅ Countersunk holes

These are sloping sided holes that will take and hide the shaped head of a screw. These are made by using a countersink drill bit rather than a twist drill bit in your hand drill. Countersink drill bits can be used on wood, plastic or metal.

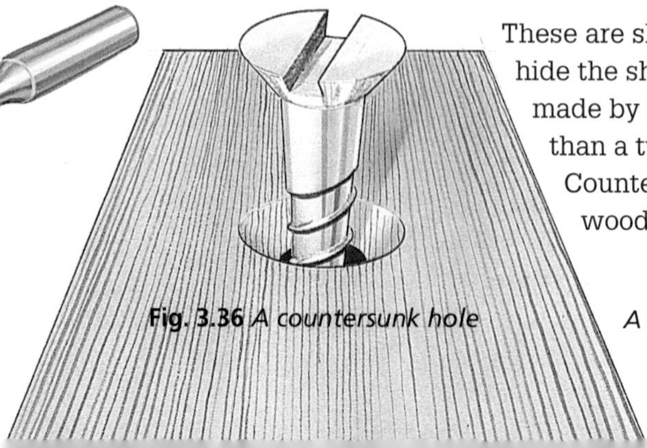

Fig. 3.35 *A forstner drill bit*

Fig. 3.36 *A countersunk hole*

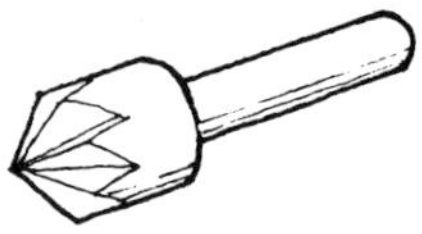

Fig. 3.37 *A countersink drill bit*

Drilling by machine ➡

Small holes can be drilled with the same twist drill bit used in hand drills, held and turned by a drilling machine. The work must be held securely, and special safety precautions must be observed. Your teacher will demonstrate the safe use of this tool. It must not be used without correct training or without your teacher's permission.

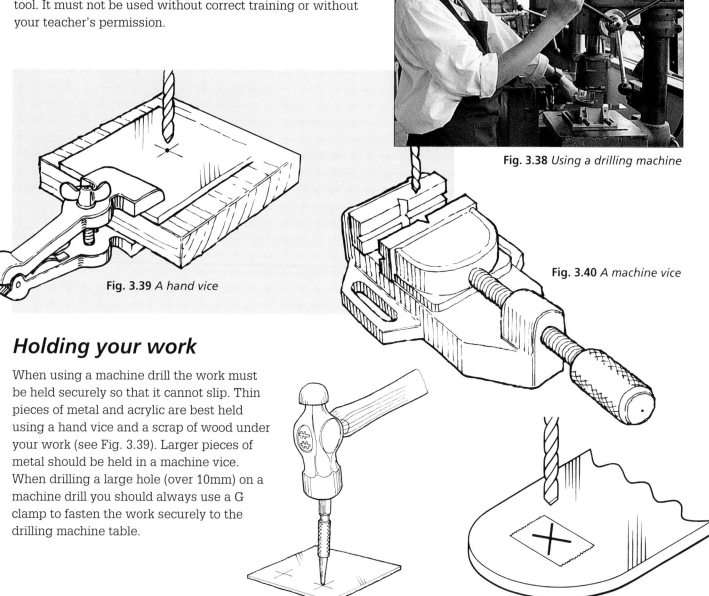

Fig. 3.38 *Using a drilling machine*

Fig. 3.39 *A hand vice*

Fig. 3.40 *A machine vice*

Holding your work

When using a machine drill the work must be held securely so that it cannot slip. Thin pieces of metal and acrylic are best held using a hand vice and a scrap of wood under your work (see Fig. 3.39). Larger pieces of metal should be held in a machine vice. When drilling a large hole (over 10mm) on a machine drill you should always use a G clamp to fasten the work securely to the drilling machine table.

Fig. 3.41 *Always use a centre punch on metal before drilling*

Fig. 3.42 *Use a marked piece of masking tape on acrylic to stop the drill slipping*

A hole saw

You can drill very large holes (14-65mm) using a hole saw fitted to a drilling machine. Your work must be held very securely with a G clamp. The hole saw cuts out a disc of wood, acrylic or metal. These discs could be used as wheels. Only use a hole saw to cut thin material.

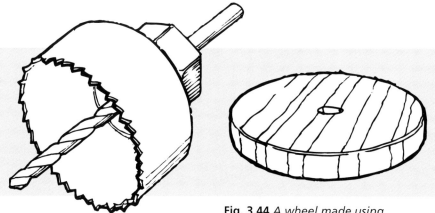

Fig. 3.43 *A hole saw*

Fig. 3.44 *A wheel made using a hole saw*

Shaping Materials

Once the large areas of waste material have been removed by sawing, the final shaping can take place. Shaping tools remove only small amounts of material. Skill is required to produce a good and true surface – and you will need to practise with these tools before you are able to use them accurately. You must choose the correct tool both for the shape that you are cutting and the material that you are using.

Fig. 3.45 *Using a plane*

Planes

Planes are mostly used on wood. They have sharp blades that cut a thin shaving off when you push them across the surface of the wood. The wood must be held firmly in a vice whilst you use the plane. Hold the plane in both hands and push along the length of the grain, changing direction if a rough surface is left (see Fig. 3.45).

The plane can be used to plane the end of a piece of wood but the wood tends to split, so care must be taken. To prevent the splitting, work from both ends towards the middle, not right across the end. Planes can also be used on acrylic. Planing the edge of an acrylic sheet produces a smooth surface but the plane requires frequent sharpening as acrylic blunts the plane blade quickly.

Planes cannot be used on metals.

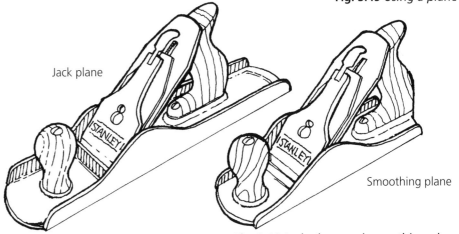

Jack plane

Smoothing plane

Fig. 3.46 *Jack plane and smoothing plane*

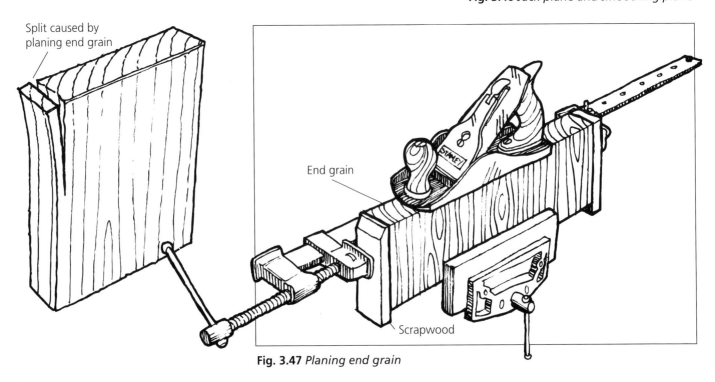

Split caused by planing end grain

End grain

Scrapwood

Fig. 3.47 *Planing end grain*

Surforms and rasps

Surforms are special file-like tools with replaceable blades. They can have flat or rounded blades. They are mainly used on wood for the rough shaping of curved shapes. Surforms cut quickly, but they tend to splinter the edges of the wood, so do take care. Thick pieces of acrylic can be shaped with care if the work is well supported. Thin acrylic will break easily if you try to shape it with a surform.

Fig. 3.48 *A surform has replaceable blades*

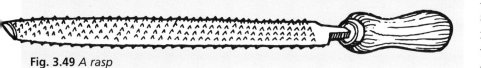

Fig. 3.49 *A rasp*

A rasp does the same job as a surform. It looks like a file, but has much rougher teeth. It is designed to cut wood quickly. It should not be used on acrylic or metal.

Chisels

Chisels are used to remove wood waste only, and they should not be used on acrylic. The blade on a chisel, which must be kept sharp, is exposed and dangerous. Chisels should therefore be carried carefully, with the blade pointing at the floor. Safety is also very important in the use of chisels. You will have to practise the technique which your teacher will show you, so that you use a chisel safely.

Here are some general rules when using a chisel:

- Always make sure your work is firmly held in a vice.
- Keep both of your hands behind the cutting blade.
- Use the correct size of chisel – the widest possible is a general rule.
- Cut across the grain where possible.
- Hit the chisel with a mallet – never use a hammer.

Fig. 3.50 *Chiselling a corner of a piece of wood*

Fig. 3.51 *Chiselling a groove across a piece of wood*

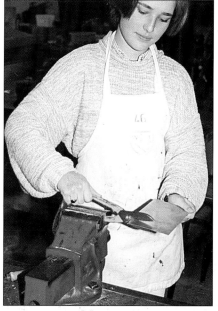

Shearing ➡

Tin snips are used in exactly the same way as scissors. They will cut thick card or thin metal. When thin metal is cut it always has a sharp edge. This edge must be smoothed with a file to round the corners slightly. This will reduce the danger of cuts. When cutting with tin snips, take care of your fingers. If you find them difficult to use, you can hold one of the handles in a vice (see Fig. 3.52). This enables you to press extra hard on the other handle, and cut more easily.

Fig. 3.52 *Using tin snips in a vice*

Filing

Files are used on both metal and plastics. Different shaped files are available to cut different shaped surfaces (see Fig. 3.54). Files also vary in the size of their teeth – the smaller the teeth, the smoother and finer the surface produced. Whatever their size, the teeth need frequent cleaning to prevent them from becoming clogged. If you rub chalk on to the file before using it, you can help prevent the file from clogging.

There are two basic methods of filing – cross-filing and draw-filing.

 Files must always be used with a correctly fitted handle. Using a file without a handle is dangerous.

Cross-filing is used to remove waste material and to file down to a line. The file is pushed across the work, which is held firmly in a vice.

Draw-filing is carried out using a smooth file to give a smooth shiny finish to the work. The file is pushed in a sideways motion up and down the edge being worked on (Fig. 3.55).

Fig. 3.53 *Using a file on acrylic*

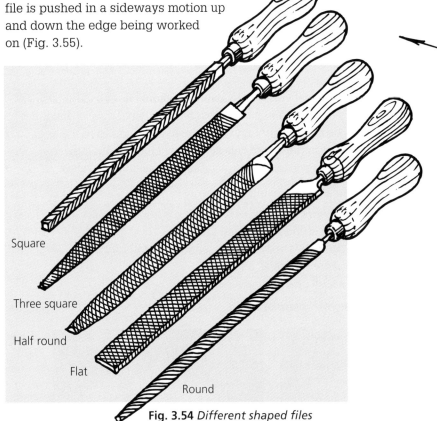

Square

Three square

Half round

Flat

Round

Fig. 3.54 *Different shaped files*

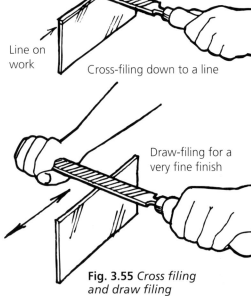

Line on work

Cross-filing down to a line

Draw-filing for a very fine finish

Fig. 3.55 *Cross filing and draw filing*

Sanding machines

A sanding machine (linisher) can be used to trim pieces of wood or plastic. It is particularly useful for trimming the end grains of pieces of wood without them splitting. A sanding machine can only be used to trim exterior or convex shapes. Use a guide set at the correct angle to hold your work against.

Fig. 3.56 *Using a sanding machine to trim a piece of wood*

Forming materials

Bending sheet metal

Sheet metal can be bent in two basic ways:

1 by folding (rather like folding card), as shown in Fig. 3.57
2 by beating into shape, to form bumps and hollows (Fig. 3.58)

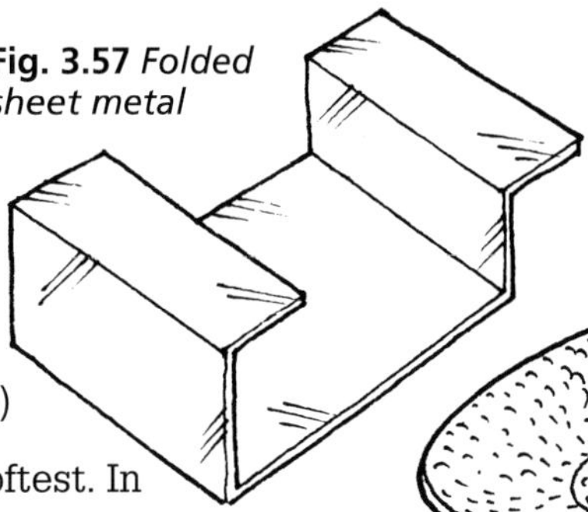

Non-ferrous metals are easiest to bend because they are the softest. In their sheet form they can be folded or beaten into shape without heating.

Where possible, folding should be undertaken using a folding press or folding bars. With small pieces of work or awkward bends, you may need to use blocks of wood to bend the work round. The basic method for folding is as follows:

1 Make sure the work is marked out clearly (Fig. 3.59a)
2 Decide the order in which to form the bends
3 Position the work carefully in the folding bars and hold it in a vice (Fig. 3.59b)
4 Using a leather mallet, or a hammer and a block of wood, bend the metal to the required angle (Fig. 3.59c).
5 Release the work from the vice and position it for forming the next bend.

Fig. 3.57 *Folded sheet metal*

Fig. 3.58 *Metal which is beaten into shape*

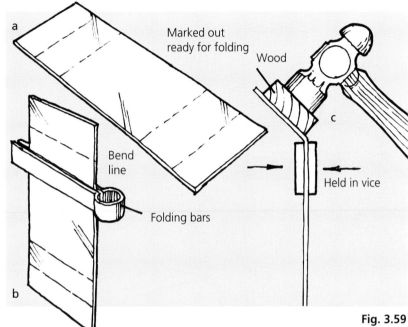

Marked out ready for folding

Wood

Bend line

Folding bars

Held in vice

Fig. 3.59

Fig. 3.60 *Using a line bender*

⚠ Remember that you must wear protective gloves when trying this.

◀ *Bending acrylic*

Plastics are easy to form and mould. When thermoplastics are softened by heating, they become very pliable. Strips of acrylic can even be tied in knots, like a ribbon, when they are hot.

Line Bending

Line bending is the simplest way to form thermoplastic, and you can make many simple shapes in acrylic by using this process:

1 Mark the position of the bend using a spirit pen or chinagraph pencil.
2 Switch on the strip heater. This is simply an electric fire element mounted below a narrow opening.
3 Place the 'bend line' that has been drawn on the work over the heat. Turn the work over every few seconds to ensure even heating (Fig. 3.60).
4 When the work gets soft along the bend line, place it on a former and hold it there until it cools. Two simple formers are shown in Figure 3.61.
5 Once cooled, the acrylic will remain bent. Remove the line you drew on it by rubbing it with metal polish.

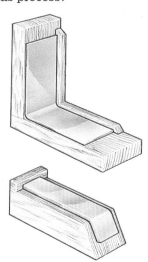

Fig. 3.61 *Formers can help you bend acrylic sccurately*

Bending metal bars ➡

Thin metal bars can be bent while cold, but thicker pieces need to be heated, using a gas torch or a forge. To get a number of bends the same a jig must be used (Fig. 3.62). You can often pull or push thin metal into shape, but you will need to use a hammer for thicker metal.

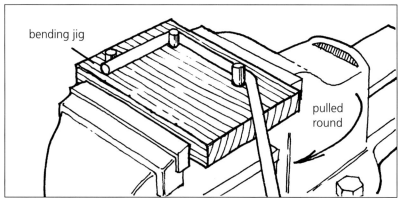

Fig. 3.62 *Simple bending jig*

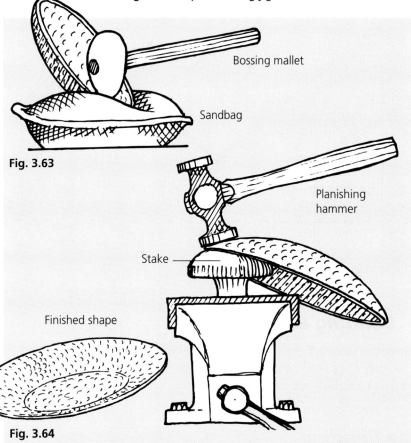

Fig. 3.63

Fig. 3.64

Forming metal

Beating is the oldest method of shaping metal. It is used a lot for decorative work and jewellery. The process is as follows:

1 Make sure the cut out shape has no sharp edges.
2 Starting at the outside edge and working in towards the centre, beat the metal to form a hollow. The work is supported on a sandbag and beaten into shape using a bossing mallet (Fig. 3.63).
3 The metal may become hardened as you work it. To soften it again you must anneal it. Annealing is done by heating the work using a gas torch and then cooling it in water.
4 Once shaped, the work must be finished by planishing. Planishing removes any lumps and bumps and hardens the metal. The work is placed on a metal planishing stake and hammered carefully, working from the centre outwards (Fig. 3.64).
5 Tidy up the edges of the work by filing.

Forming plastic

Press forming

The temperature that is required to soften acrylic is around 160°C. This can be achieved by using an oven set at the correct temperature. (Remember to wear protective gloves.) Acrylic cools slowly, because it is a poor conductor of heat. It assumes the shape that it has been formed in when hot. Pressing the acrylic into a mould when soft can produce many different shapes – dishes and containers can be made very easily. A two-part former can be used to mould the acrylic (see Fig. 3.65). The mould must not be opened, however, until the acrylic is cool or it will not freeze into the new shape. The moulded acrylic can then be trimmed, if required.

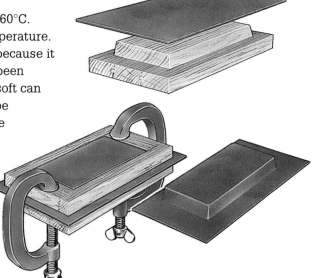

Fig. 3.65 *Using a two-part press former*

Vacuum forming

Vacuum forming is another method of shaping plastics, using a special machine (see Fig. 3.66). The plastic sheet is heated evenly until soft, and then air pressure is used to shape it over a mould. The heating element is similar to the grill on a cooker and is usually movable to allow access to the machine. The sheet of plastic, acrylic or high density polystyrene is fixed across the top of the machine by clamping. This must form an airtight seal. Below the plastic sheet in the air chamber is the mould (Fig. 3.67). When the sheet is hot and soft, the heater is moved, the mould is raised and the air between the mould and the plastic sheet is evacuated by an air pump.

Fig. 3.66

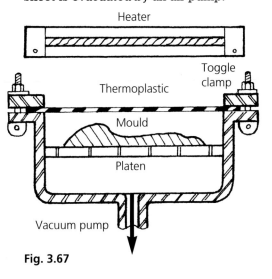

Fig. 3.67

The air pressure on the outside of the sheet then presses the plastic into close contact with the mould. The shape of the mould must be carefully designed to allow the plastic sheet to be easily removed, and the mould reused. Vacuum-formed components always have a shell of the same thickness throughout. This method of construction is extensively used in the packaging industry. Most food packaging and other small containers are formed by his method. Much larger machines are used to form acrylic baths, for use in houses.

Injection moulding

Plastics can be shaped by forcing softened plastic into a specially shaped hole and allowing it to set. This process is called injection moulding. Many plastic items are produced by this method, including plastic kits for making model boats, cars, planes etc. In these kits you can see the runners joining lots of small parts together. This is where the plastic has been forced into the mould. It is possible in a school workshop to produce small wheels and other items by injection moulding. It is not easy, however, to make the moulds for this process because they must be made from metal.

Injection-moulded components often have a complex shape and can range from being small to being very large. One of the largest injection mouldings is the hull of a Topper dinghy used in sailing schools (see Fig. 3.68).

Fig. 3.68

Hot forming metal

Forging

Hot forging is one of the oldest methods of working iron and steel. It involves heating the metal to a bright red colour and then beating it into shape on an anvil. In school chip forges are used to heat the metal. Figs 3.70 and 3. 71 show the stages in producing a loop on the end of a rod and the stages in the production of a simple scroll.

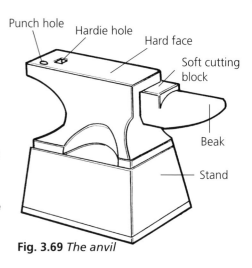

Fig. 3.69 *The anvil*

1 Measure distance and mark
with a punch

πd or 3.14 × diameter

2 Bend to a
right angle

3 Turn the
end over

4

5

6

7 Close
the loop

Fig. 3.70 *Forming a loop in a rod*

⚠ Danger handling hot metal needs care.

1 Draw
down — Red heat

2 Flatten
and taper

3 Start scroll by
turning over
the tip

4 Continue
by rolling-
up the face

5 Use horns
to form
the scroll — Vice

6 A scroll tool
can be used
to complete
the scroll — Vice

Scroll tool

3.71 *Forming a scroll in a strip of metal*

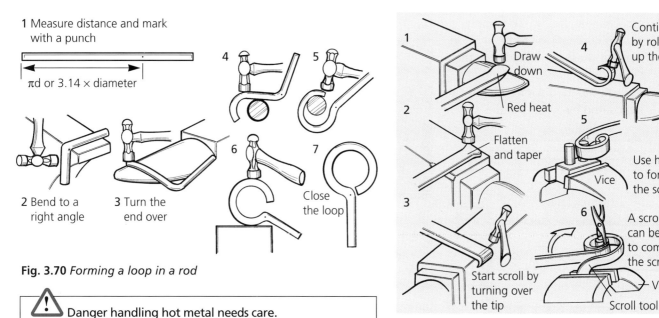

Laminated salad servers

Pressure – vice or sash cramps

Laminates

Veneers

Wax layer

Wax

Paper/polythene

Waxed hardwood clamping blocks

Base board   Laminates

Construction leg unit
(tables/chairs)

Fig. 3.72 *Laminating wood using clamp pressure and shaped formers to shape veneers*

Forming wood

To produce shapes in wood that are strong the grain of the wood must be considered. If the grain lines are long the shape will be strong. However, if the grain lines are short the shape will break easily.

Laminating

Forming wood by bending can produce strong shapes.

However, it is difficult to bend thick pieces of wood. An answer is to use thin layers of wood (veneers) that can be bent easily. The layers are glued together and placed in a shaped former or jig. When the glue is set the shaped wood can be removed and used.

Re-forming materials

Intricate shapes can be made by re-forming metals. This involves melting them and then pouring them into shaped moulds and allowing them to set by cooling. Very little material is wasted using this method as the 'waste' can be melted and re-used.

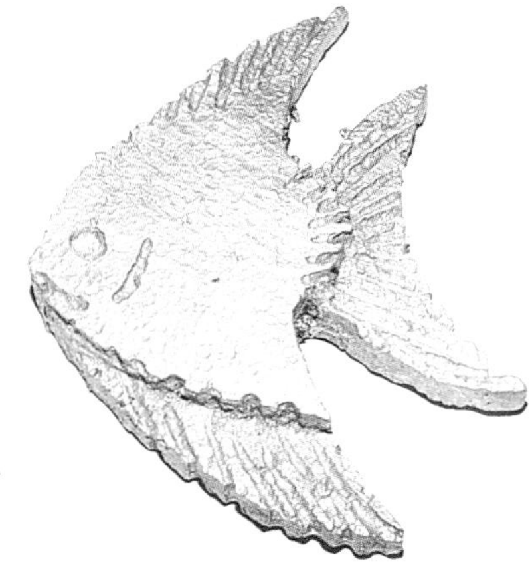

Some plastics can also be re-formed. In this case, the material starts off as a liquid and is mixed with chemicals which cause it to change from a liquid to a solid and assume the shape of the mould it has been poured into.

Casting metal

Casting was one of the earliest methods of shaping metal to be used. It is still used a lot today, for making things like car engines, machine parts and vices. In D&T most casting is done using aluminium, which melts easily and is easy to work with.

There are three stages in casting:

1 Making the pattern
2 Making the mould
3 Making the casting

Making a pattern ➡

A pattern is an exact copy of the shape you want to make. If you only want to make one casting you can use expanded polystyrene, which will be destroyed when the molten metal is poured on it (see Fig. 3.74). If you want to make several castings then you need to make a pattern that you can use again and again - most are made from wood.

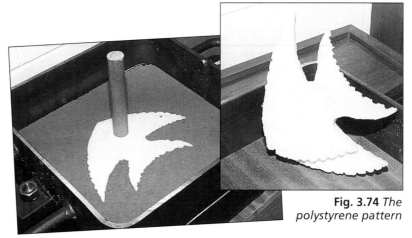

Fig. 3.73 *A decorative wall hanging made by re-forming metal*

Fig. 3.74 *The polystyrene pattern*

Fig. 3.75 *Pattern and runner in mould*

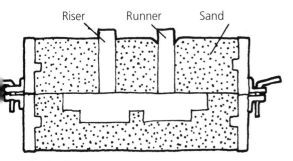

Riser   Runner   Sand

Fig. 3.76

Making a mould

The pattern is placed in a casting box and is packed in sand (see Fig. 3.76). You need to make a way in for the molten metal by including a runner, and, riser to provide an escape route for excess metal. When packing the casting box. If you are using a wooden pattern, you must separate the two parts of the casting box and take the pattern out, leaving the hole in its place as the mould. When using the expanded polystyrene pattern you can leave the pattern in the sand – it will be destroyed when the molten metal is poured on it.

Making a casting

At school you will probably use polystyrene patterns when you make a metal casting. When the molten metal is poured into the runner (your teacher will do this for you) the metal flows into the mould rapidly burning out the expanded polystyrene and replacing it. The riser is also burnt out and allows gases and fumes to escape from the mould. The casting must now be left to cool before opening the mould. Remember that the runner and the riser must be cut off before final shaping.

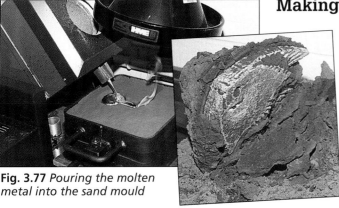

Fig. 3.77 *Pouring the molten metal into the sand mould*

Fig. 3.78 *The casting is opened when it has cooled*

Shaping materials

Using a lathe

A lathe is a machine tool that rotates your work while a tool cuts away the waste material. Lathes can be used to shape wood, metal and other resistant materials.

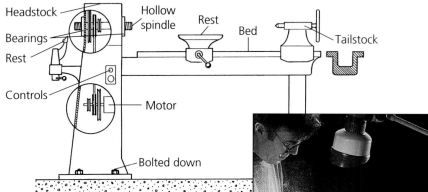

Fig. 3.80 *A wood turning lathe*

Fig. 3.79 *Items made from turned wood*

Wood turning lathe

A wood turning lathe can be used to create wooden bowls and similar hollowed objects. It can also be used to make spindle type objects such as chair legs or baseball bats (see Fig. 3.80).

Turning bowls

Turning a bowl involves screwing the wood to a metal plate called a face plate, which is fastened to the outside spindle. The waste wood is cut away using chisels and scrapers.

Turning spindles

For spindles, the wood is held between a forked centre in the inside spindle of the lathe and a fixed centre in the tailstock. The work is gripped and turned by the forked centre. The cutting tools should be held firmly against the tool rest while the wood rotates against them.

Fig. 3.82 *Turning a bowl on a lathe*

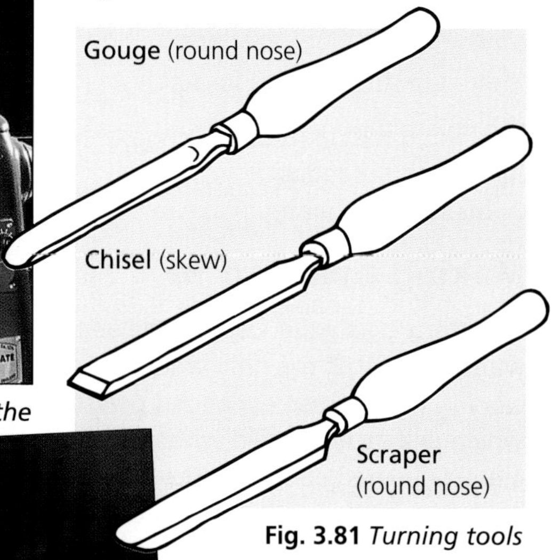

Fig. 3.81 *Turning tools*

Fig. 3.83 *Turning a spindle on a wood lathe*

Engineering lathe

The engineering lathe (centre lathe) is used to machine metal components to give a smooth and accurate surface. In industry mass produced components such as nuts and bolts are made on a lathe, although rather different from those used in the school workshop. Industrial lathes are often controlled by computer which means that once they are set up they will produce items with very little engineer support.

The work is held in a gripping device called a chuck and the tool is fixed securely to the lathe. The tool can be moved along or across an axis by turning handles. This enables very accurate movement of the tool, allowing for very accurate pieces to be produced. Metal can get very hot when being cut on a lathe. To stop the tool becoming too hot to cut properly cooling fluids are used.

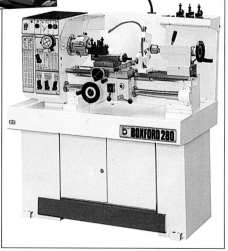

Fig. 3.84 *An engineering lathe*

⚠️ Goggles must be worn when using lathes.
All guards must be in place.
Do not use machines without permission and training.

Computer aided manufacture

Computers are used to help with the manufacture of many different products. In the school workshop you may come across machines that are controlled by computer. The most common are cutter/plotters and engraving cutters. You may also find computer-controlled lathes and milling machines. They all work in a similar way. Firstly the component is drawn on the computer using a drafting program, then the computer controls the cutting tool to produce component that matches the drawing.

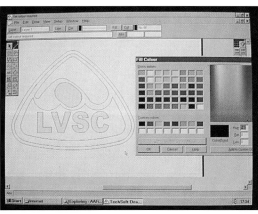

Fig. 3.85 *Logo on screen*

Cutter/Plotter (CAMM1)

This machine can either draw with a pen (plotter) or can be fitted with a knife to cut out shapes in vinyl laminate (Fig. 3.86). Any shape that can be drawn on the screen can be cut out. This enables the production of very accurate and professional letters, logos and numbers (Fig. 3.87).

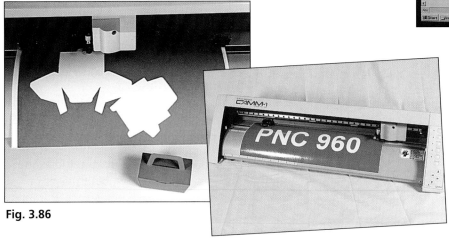

Fig. 3.86

Fig. 3.87

Engraver (CAMM2)

Here the computer controls the movement of a rotating cutter. This machine will produce signs by cutting two tone laminated plastics using a vee cutter to penetrate the first coloured layer to show the lower colour. Fitted with a small drill, it can be used to cut out very complex shapes from acrylic sheet (to produce these shapes by hand would require a very high level of skill with a range of saws and files). This tool can also be used with appropriate software to produce printed circuit boards by engraving, rather than by etching in acid.

Write down the most useful features of a machine used for computer-aided manufacture.

Fig. 3.88 *Many articles can be produced using CAMM2*

Fig. 3.89 *Cutting a toast rack from acrylic sheet*

Fig. 3.90 *Cutting a printed circuit board*

Joining wood

Box joints

Boxes of various shapes and sizes are the basis of many things made in wood. They range from small pencil boxes to bookcases and wardrobes. The joints on a box can be made in many different ways some of the basic ways are shown below.

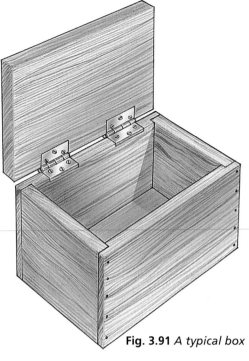

Fig. 3.91 *A typical box*

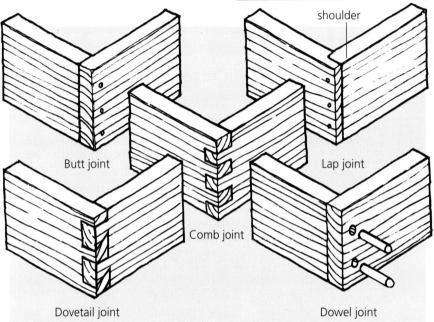

Fig. 3.92 *The different types of box joint*

Corners

The butt joint is the simplest joint to use as with all joints, both pieces of wood need to be cut accurately. It has no mechanical strength of its own and relies entirely on glue and nails.

The lap joint has a shoulder which gives it a little more rigidity than the butt joint. Like the butt joint it relies on glue and nails for its strength.

A dowel joint does have mechanical strength, because the wooden peg (dowel) goes into both pieces of wood. Glue adds further strength.

A comb joint is an interlocking joint which, when well made and glued has a lot of srength.

A dovetail joint is more complicated and difficult to make than the others described, but if it is well made and glued, it is very strong.

Partitions

It is often necessary to divide a box into sections. There are three ways of doing this.

The butt joint, again is the simplest method. It must be accurately made and relies on glue and nails for its strength.

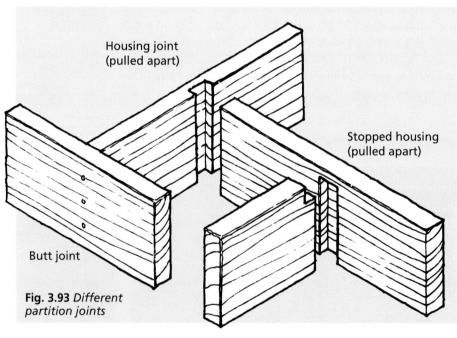

Fig. 3.93 *Different partition joints*

A housing joint is a much stronger joint. Like all joints, it needs to be cut carefully and to fit well if it is to have maximum strength. It can be glued in, or glued and nailed.

A stopped housing joint involves more work than the other two, but gives a neater looking joint, it is normally glued together.

Frame joints

Frames are used when making stools, chairs or doors. The joints can be made in many ways. Some of the more common ways are shown below.

The halving joint is the simplest frame joint . It has no mechanical strength and relies on glue and screws or wooden pegs (dowels) for its strength.

The bridle joint is an interlocking joint, which when glued is very strong. It is important to get the thickness of each piece right so as not to weaken the joint.

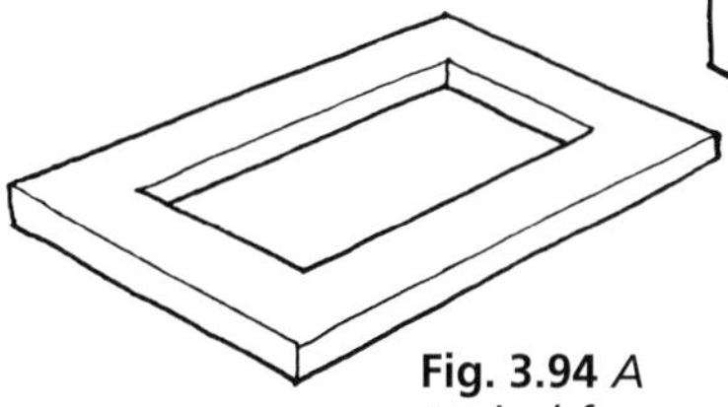

The mortice and tenon joint is the strongest of all the frame joints. It is also neater in appearance. When glued together, none of the joints show. This type of joint is often found on stools, chairs and tables.

The dowel joint is a strong joint, especially when glued. It is commonly used in industrial furniture making. When making dowel joints by hand it can be difficult to drill the holes accurately. Not only do they have to be in the correct position but they have to be straight. If they are not accurate the joint will not fit together.

Accurate drilling can only be achieved by using a drilling jig. This guides the drill, making sure the holes are straight and in the right position.

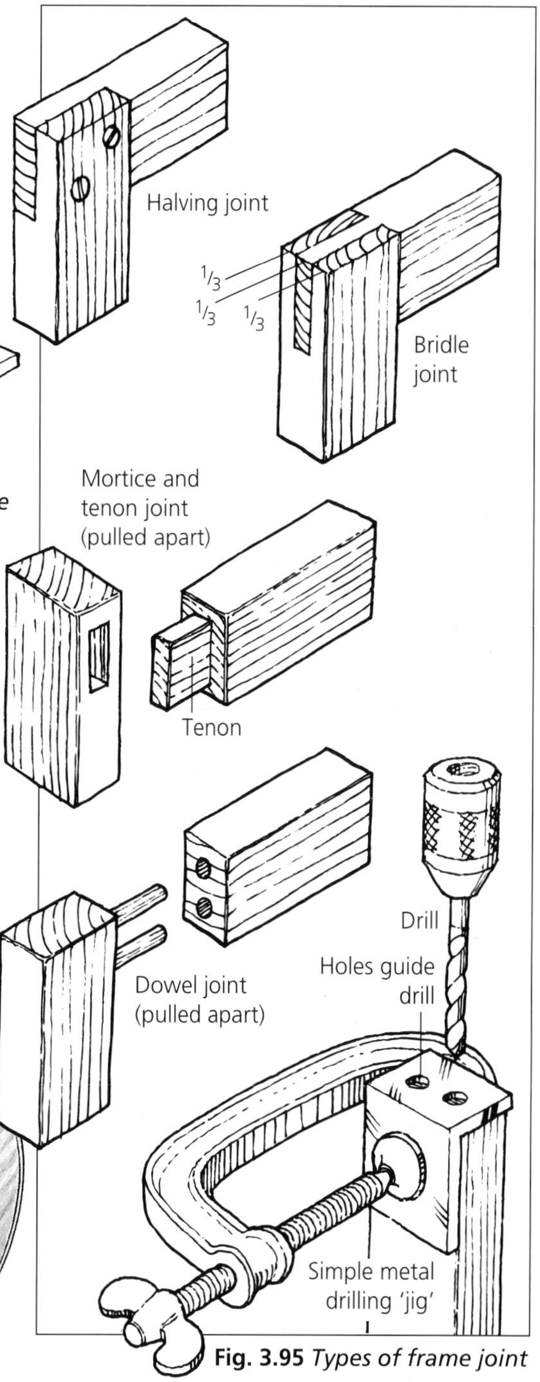

Rotating and sliding parts

Many of your projects will require you to make parts that will rotate, such as wheels. The wheel is held in place by two arms, one at each side, that are fixed. The axle is fastened to the wheel with glue and is free to turn in the holes in each of the arms.

Fig. 3.94 *A typical frame*

Halving joint

Bridle joint

Mortice and tenon joint (pulled apart)

Tenon

Dowel joint (pulled apart)

Drill

Holes guide drill

Simple metal drilling 'jig'

Fig. 3.96 *A freely rotating wheel*

Fig. 3.95 *Types of frame joint*

Alternatively, the axle could be fixed on the arms with glue, and the wheel left to turn freely on the axle.

Boxes can have sliding lids if grooves are cut in the sides, near the top. You must remember to cut the grooves before joining the box together. Plywood or acrylic are suitable materials to use as sliding box lids.

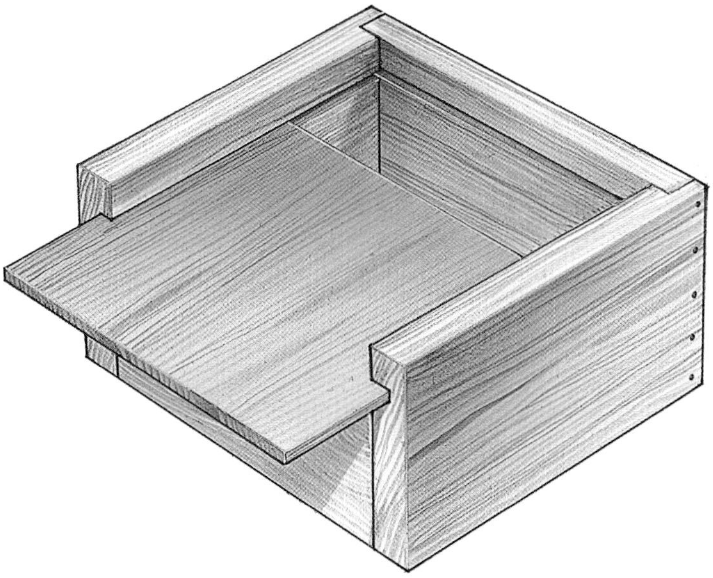

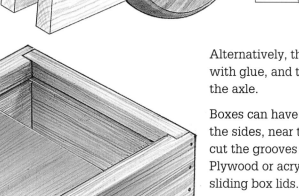

Fig. 3.97 *A box with a sliding lid*

Nails

Nails and pins provide a permanent method of joining wood. Nails grip by friction: the fibres hold the nail in place. Nails are usually made of mild steel and come in different shapes and sizes (Fig. 3.98).

You should nail together pieces of wood as follows:

1 Choose the correct type of nail for the job. Its length should be two or three times the thickness of the wood it is holding down.
2 Knock the nail into the top piece so that the tip is just showing through the bottom of it.
3 If gluing the joint, apply the glue now.
4 Place the parts together and knock in the nails.
5 Punch the nails below the surface.
6 Put filler in the holes and allow to dry.

Type of nail	Uses
Round wire 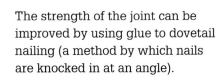	Used for cheap construction work; the heads cannot be punched below the surface.
Oval wire	Used for better quality work; the heads can be punched below the surface. Filler is used to cover the holes.
Panel pin	Used for fixing thin sheet material or small butt and lap joints. The head can easily be punched below the surface.

Fig. 3.98

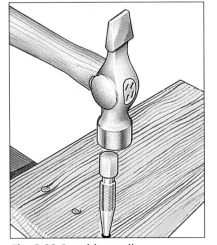

Fig. 3.99 *Punching nails below the surface*

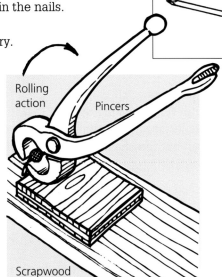

Fig. 3.100 *Removing a bent nail*

The strength of the joint can be improved by using glue to dovetail nailing (a method by which nails are knocked in at an angle).

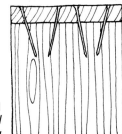

Fig. 3.101 *Dovetail nailing*

Screws

Wood screws provide a stronger joint than nails. They cut their way into the lower piece of wood becoming enmeshed with the wood fibres and pulling the joint together. They are all the same basic shape, but they have different types of head and can be made from different types of metal.

Use wood screws as follows:

1 Choose the correct screw. It should be two to three times longer than the top piece of wood is thick.
2 Drill a clearance hole in the top piece of wood . Its diameter should be slightly larger than the shank of the screw.
3 If you are using a countersunk screw, drill a countersink to allow the head to lie just below the wood surface.
4 Make a pilot hole in the lower piece of wood. The hole must be thinner than the screw so that the screw will cut into the sides of it.
5 Insert the screw with the correct screwdriver.

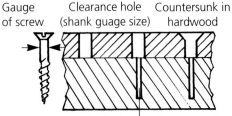

Gauge of screw   Clearance hole (shank guage size)   Countersunk in hardwood

Pilot hole core diameter   **Fig. 3.103** *Preparation for fixing screws*

Type of screw	Uses
Countersunk	Most common general purpose screw, they are used to join wood to wood and to fit hinges and brackets. The head fits flush to the surface.
Round head	Used to attach fittings to wood, e.g. tee hinges and brackets and sheet materials.
Raised head	Used to attach fittings to wood. Often plated with chrome or made of brass.
Pozidrive head	Used with a special pozidrive screwdriver. Their advantage is that the screwdriver grips better, making a slip less likely.

Fig. 3.102 *The most common types of wood screw*

Gluing

Most joints between two pieces of wood can be strengthened by using glue.

Some joints rely solely on the glue to hold interlocking pieces together. Other joints use a combination of nails or screws and glue. Glued joints are permanent joints.

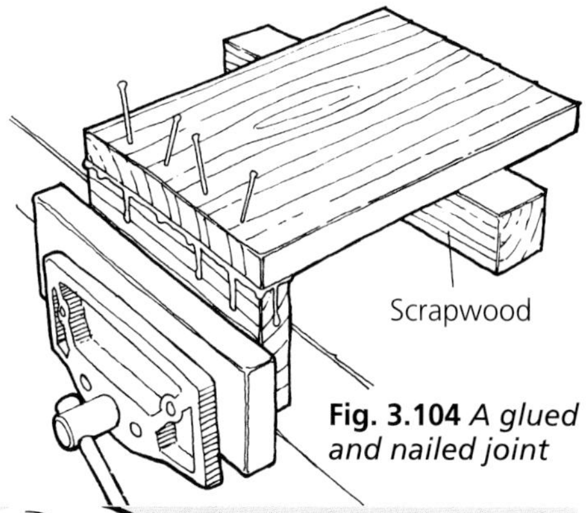

Glued and nailed joints

Fig. 3.104 shows a butt joint in position ready for nailing. Use the following procedure for this type of joint.

1 Hold one piece securely in a vice.
2 Get the nails started in the other (top) piece of wood.
3 Put a thin layer of glue on both touching surfaces.
4 Position and hammer in nails.
5 Wipe off any excess glue, using a damp paper towel.

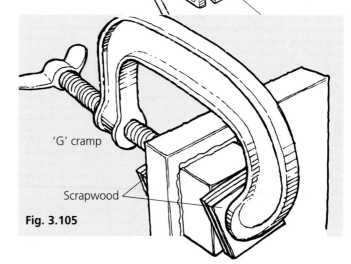

Scrapwood

Fig. 3.104 A glued and nailed joint

'G' cramp

Scrapwood

Fig. 3.105

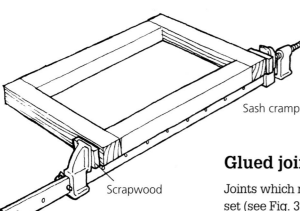

Sash cramp

Scrapwood

Fig. 3.106 *Gluing using a sash cramp*

Glued joints

Joints which rely solely on glue have to be held firmly together until the glue has set (see Fig. 3.105). For making successful joints use the following procedure.

1 Make sure the joint is a good fit to start with (i.e. with no large gaps to fill).
2 Get your cramps ready and adjust them to the required size.
3 Collect pieces of scrapwood to put between the cramp and your work.
4 Put a thin layer of glue on both touching surfaces.
5 Push the parts together by hand.
6 Put the cramp on, placing the piece of scrapwood between your work and the cramp.
7 Tighten the cramp and wipe off excessive glue .
8 Leave until the joint is set then remove the cramps.

Wood glues

PVA

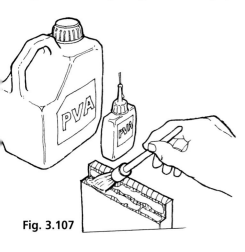

Fig. 3.107

This is the most common type of glue used. It is a white creamy liquid derived from a plastic called PVA (polyvinlyacetate). It can be spread neatly onto a joint using a brush (see Fig. 3.107). Do not spread it too thinly as it will tend to soak into the wood. Once the joint has been nailed or cramped any excess glue should be wiped off with a damp paper towel. It is extremely difficult to remove excess glue once it has set (the setting time is about 4 hours). Waterproof and non-waterproof types of PVA are available for both outdoors and indoor use.

Glue gun

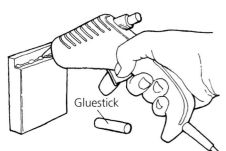

Gluestick

Fig. 3.108 *Using a glue gun*

These are electrically powered. They heat up a solid stick of glue and melt it. When the trigger is pressed, the melted glue comes out of the nozzle. The glue used in a glue gun sets very quickly (in less than a minute). It is only practical for use on small areas. It will stick other materials as well as wood.

Joining Metal

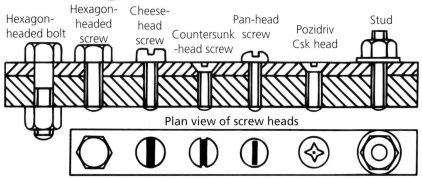

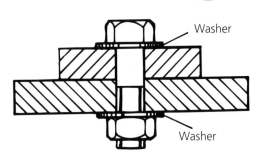

Fig. 3.109 *Machine screws*

Machine screws, nuts and bolts

Machine screws, nuts and bolts are a convenient method of joining materials together. They are easily undone and are suitable for all kinds and combinations of materials.

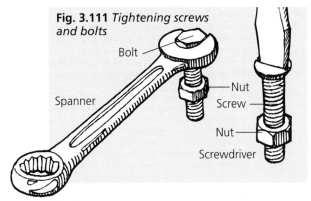

Fig. 3.111 *Tightening screws and bolts*

Fig. 3.110 *Nut and bolt*

Machine screws

Machine screws (set screws) are threaded for the whole of their length. They are used to secure components together. The top piece of the material must have a clearance hole through which the screw will pass. The lower piece of material to which it is being fastened has a thread cut to grip the screw. Machine screws are made with various types of head: screwdriver slot, pozidrive slot, or a hexagonal head.

Bolts

Bolts are similar to machine screws except that the thread stops before it reaches the head. This unthreaded part allows the bolt to fit more closely in the clearance hole providing a better mechanical fixing. The bolt is fastened with a nut to fix the parts together, rather than a thread being made in the material.

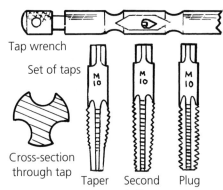

Self tapping screws ➡

Self tapping screws are suitable for fixing together thin sheets of metal. Preparation involves drilling a clearance hole and a pilot hole, equal to the screw's core diameter (see Fig. 3.112).

Making screw threads

It is necessary to cut a screw thread in metal or acrylic when using machine screws. An internal thread is cut using a screw tap. Three taps are available for each size of thread (Fig. 3.113). A hole is drilled, called a tapping size hole, smaller than the screw size. The tap, held in a taprench, (see Fig. 3.114) is then gently turned in the hole and cuts a spiral thread in the material. The cutting sequence involves turning the tap clockwise for half a turn then anticlockwise for a quarter turn to break the swarf.

Fig. 3.112

Fig. 3.113 *Tapping drill sizes*

Nominal Diameter	Pitch (mm)	Tapping drill size (mm)
M4	0.7	3.3
M5	0.8	4.2
M6	1.0	5.0
M8	1.25	6.8
M10	1.5	8.5

Fig. 3.114 *Taps and tap wrench*

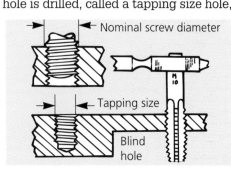

Fig. 3.115 *Tapping*

Rivets and riveting

Riveting is a quick method of fixing two or more pieces of material together in a permanent fashion. The choice of rivet depends on its use. Rivets can form hinge pins in moving joints, or rigid joints in sheet material. Rivets are made from soft, easily formed metals such as iron, brass and aluminium. Aluminium rivets are suitable for joining acrylic sheet, but minimum force must be used to avoid cracking the material.

Countersunk riveting

A countersunk rivet is used when a smooth surface is required. It is very strong and neat when filed smooth. Figure 3.116 shows the sequence of operation required to fit a countersunk rivet.

Snap-head riveting

Snap-head riveting is used for fastening pieces of material that are too thin to allow countersinking. They are also used for decorative reasons on wrought ironwork. Fig. 3.117 shows the sequence of operations required to fit a snap-head rivet.

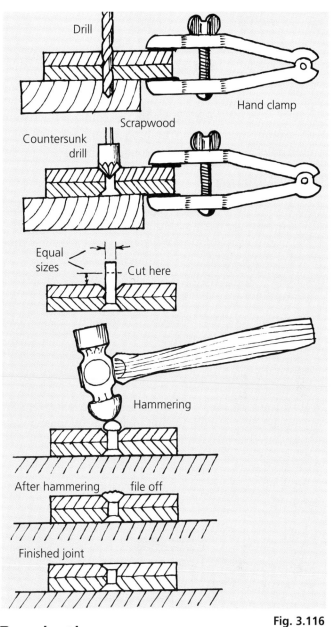

Fig. 3.116

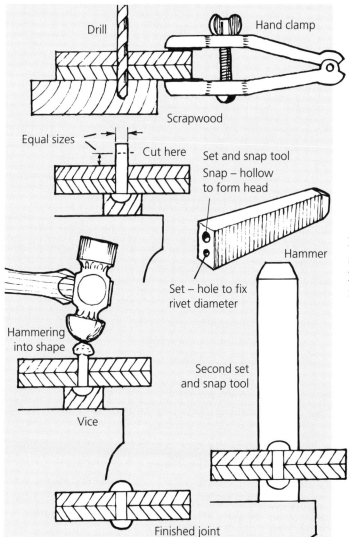

Fig. 3.117

Pop riveting

Pop riveting is quick and easy, and can be done from one side of the work. Pop rivets always leave a protruding head. The process is shown in the sequence Figure 3.118. A special tool is required to complete the joint.

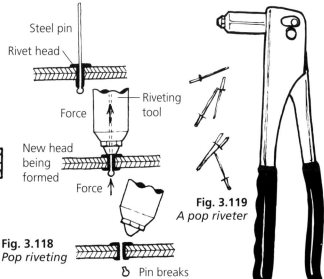

Fig. 3.118
Pop riveting

Fig. 3.119
A pop riveter

Soldering

Soldering makes a permanent joint between two pieces of metal. It can be used on steel, tin plate, brass or copper. It cannot be used on aluminium. There are two types of soldering: soft soldering and hard soldering. The two types use different metals for the solder, which melt at different temperatures. The higher temperature used in hard soldering produces a stronger joint.

Soft soldering

Soft soldering uses a solder which is a mixture of tin and lead. It is soft and melts at around 230°C. There are two methods of soft soldering. One is used when joining sheet metals and the other is used when fixing electronic components into a circuit. (See page 85 for this method.) Use soft solder for sheet metal as follows:

1 Make sure the joint is a good fit and clean. Do not touch the metal after cleaning.
2 Flux around the joint. Flux is a liquid or paste which keeps the metal clean when heating. Use Bakers fluid on steel.
3 Heat the joint gently. Touch the solder to the joint. The end of the solder should melt and run into the joint.
4 Leave to cool without moving the joint.
5 Wash off the flux and dry thoroughly.

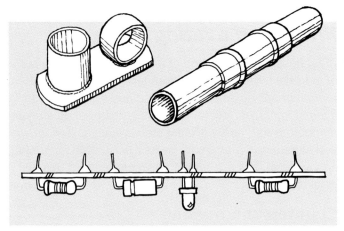

Fig. 3.120 *Soldered joints*

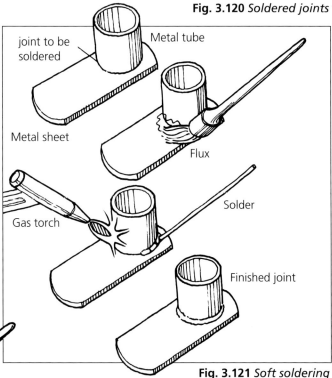

Fig. 3.121 *Soft soldering*

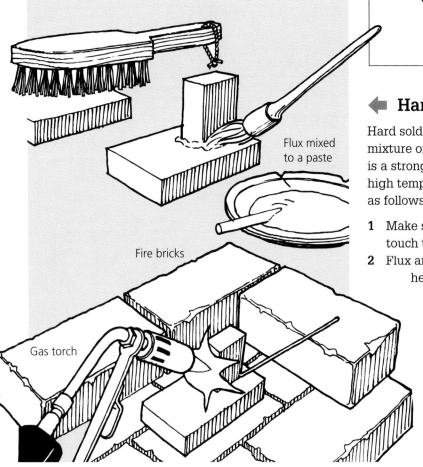

◀ Hard soldering (brazing)

Hard soldering is only used on steel. The solder is a mixture of copper and zinc and melts at around 960°C. It is a strong method of joining steel but requires a very high temperature, so care must be taken. The process is as follows:

1 Make sure the joint is a good fit and clean. Do not touch the metal after cleaning.
2 Flux around the joint to keep the metal clean when heating. Use borax powder as the flux, and mix it to a thick paste.
3 Position firebricks around the joint so that they reflect the heat.
4 Heat the joint gently at first to boil off the water in the flux.
5 Heat the metal strongly to a very bright red. Touch the solder to the joint. The end of the solder should melt and run into the joint.
6 Leave to cool without moving the joint.

Fig. 3.122 *Hard soldering*

Joining plastic

Plastics particularly acrylic, can be joined to wood and metal with screws or nuts and bolts. You have to take care not to tighten the screws too much or the acrylic will crack, Figs. 3.123 & 3.124 show acrylic joined in various ways. Joining two pieces of plastic together cannot really be done in the same sort of way, because the material is often very thin or not strong enough. The only practical possibility is to glue them together.

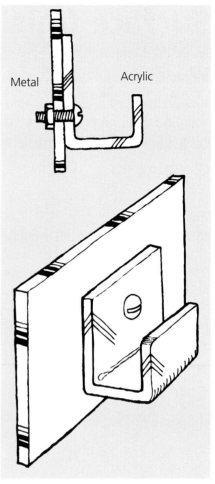

Metal   Acrylic

Fig. 3.124 *Acrylic bolted on to metal*

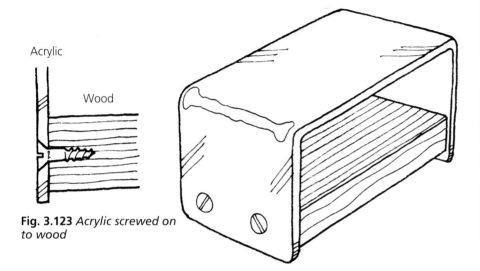

Acrylic

Wood

Fig. 3.123 *Acrylic screwed on to wood*

Gluing Plastics

If you use the wrong glue for a particular plastic, you may find that the plastic melts. If you are unsure about which glue to use for a particular plastic, try some glue out on bits of waste material first. Epoxy resin glues such as Araldite Rapid, can be used on most plastics. However, in some situations, a different glue might be more effective. Epoxy resin glues work quite well on acrylic, but the best glues to use on acrylic are the special acrylic glues, such as Tensol Cement. Use Tensol Cement as follows:

1 Make sure the joint is a good fit.
2 Make sure the joint is really clean. Wash it with soapy water, rinse in fresh water and dry it on a clean paper towel.
3 Put the glue very carefully onto the work. Try not to get the glue anywhere else – it is difficult to get off.
4 Apply pressure to the joint for 5 or 10 minutes until it has set.

⚠ Caution – the fumes given off by glue are unpleasant. Replace the lid immediately after use and work in a well ventilated area.

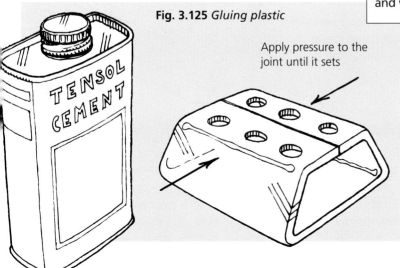

Fig. 3.125 *Gluing plastic*

Apply pressure to the joint until it sets

Fixing with screws

Screws can be used to join some of the softer plastics, such as PVC (polyvinyl chloride). Self-tapping screws are best for this, as they cut their own thread into the plastic once a pilot hole has been drilled. For details of using self-tapping screws see page 60.

Fig. 3.126 *Self-tapping screw*

Surface finishes

Wood

Finishes are applied to wood to give it an attractive, surface and to protect it from the effects of moisture. If a piece of wood gets damp it will swell and begin to rot.

Cleaning up

First of all the wood must be made clean and smooth, ready for the finish to be applied.

1 Hold the work firmly in a vice and, using a smoothing plane, plane along the grain removing only very thin shavings. This cleans the surface of the wood.
2 Using a piece of glass paper wrapped around a sanding block, rub along the grain to smooth the wood. Start with coarse grade and move to a fine grade for final rubbing.

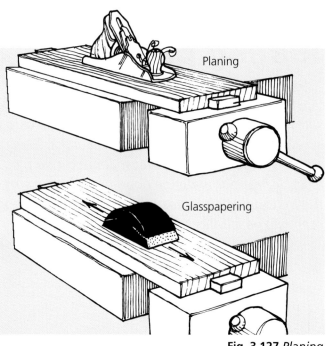

Fig. 3.127 *Planing*

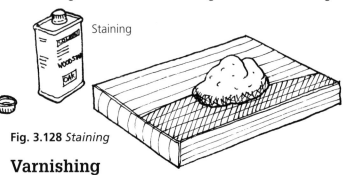

Fig. 3.128 *Staining*

Staining

If you want to change the colour of a piece of wood, you should use a stain straight after cleaning up. The stain will not obstruct the view of the wood grain. Stains come in many colours. They are applied using a cloth, working along the grain. A stain will not protect the wood from the damp.

Varnishing

A varnish will protect your work from the damp and allow you to see through to the wood grain below. Varnish your work as follows:

1 Brush the varnish on , working along the grain. Only have a little varnish on the brush. Brush from the centre of the work towards the ends.
2 Leave to dry overnight.
3 Rub the surface down very gently with fine glasspaper, until it feels smooth.
4 Add another coat of varnish and leave to dry.
5 If it is still rough after the second coat, rub down again and apply a third coat of varnish (see Fig. 3.129).

Fig. 3.129

Painting

Painting is used to apply colours to a surface. When it is done well the grain of the wood does not show through. For the best results, use polyurethane gloss paints. The process of painting is similar to varnishing. Apply special primer paint first to seal the wood.

Plastic

The majority of plastics do not need any extra surface finish. They already have an extremely good surface finish from the forming process. The edges, however, will have to be smoothed and polished. Smooth and polish as follows:

1 Hold your work firmly in a vice. Protect the already polished surfaces using paper or pieces of wood. Drawfile the edge, using a smooth file until all the scratches have been removed.

2 Rub the edge with 'wet and dry' paper to remove all the file marks. Dip the paper in water as you use it.

3 Polish the edge with Brasso or a special perspex polish. Use a cloth and rub very hard, or use a buffing machine under the supervision of the teacher.

Metal

Metals require finishing both to protect and to enhance them. All metals react with the oxygen and moisture in the air which will oxidise (corrode) the surface. Steel is corroded easily and as a result, rust, is clearly visible on car bodies and old metal fences. Copper oxidises and turns greeny brown when exposed to the air. Gold does not oxidise, so that jewellery made from gold does not need to be polished very often.

Bright metal finish (polishing)

All metals can be polished. The first stage is to produce a smooth surface. This is done by removing saw marks with a file, then removing the file marks with a coarse emery cloth, and using finer grades of emery until the surface is clear of imperfections and a dull, matt surface has been achieved. This is not a fast process and requires patience to produce good results.

The next stage involves using fine grade polishing compounds. They are rubbed on the surface using a buffing machine (see Fig. 3.130).

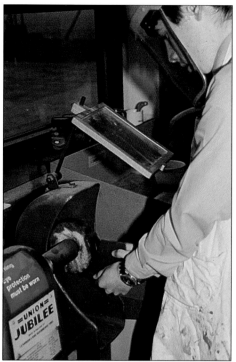

Fig. 3.130 *Using a buffing machine*

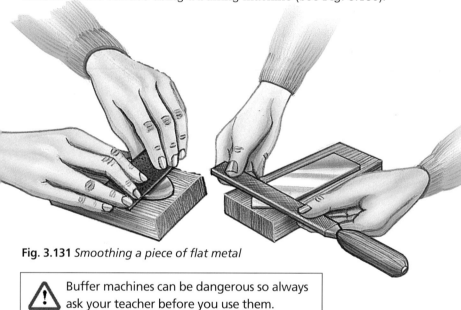

Fig. 3.131 *Smoothing a piece of flat metal*

> ⚠ Buffer machines can be dangerous so always ask your teacher before you use them.

The final stage is carried out to protect the metal from the air. Steel can be heated until blue and oil is smeared on the hot surface, this is called bluing. When cool the surface of the steel is rubbed with an oily rag. This protection can be extended by occasionally oiling with a rag. Steel, brass, copper, and aluminium can be coated with a clear laquer, that protects but allows the metal colour to show. This is a suitable finish for 'clean' articles.

Painting

Metals can be painted to protect them from the air, in a similar manner to wood. The surface must be smooth and clean and free from oil and grease. Metal paints such as Hammerite require only one coat to fully protect the metal. Many different colours are available. The colour of the metal is not visible through the painted surface, therefore metals such as copper, brass gold and silver are not often painted.

← Plastic coating

Steel can be coated in a plastic layer to protect and enhance its surface. First the metal is smoothed and cleaned as if for polishing (but not as smooth). The metal is then heated to about 180°C in an oven, and dipped in plastic coating powder, preferably in a fluidisation tank (see Fig. 3.132). An alternative is to carefully sprinkle the dust over the surface). The powder will stick to the hot metal. If the metal is returned to the oven and reheated for a few minutes the plastic becomes smooth and glossy. When removed from the oven it should be hung up carefully to cool. The plastic is very hot and will remain so for a long time. This finish is suitable for handles on small tools, racks, and is used in industry to coat wire baskets such as those used for fridge racks.

Dip coated workpiece

Fluidised plastic

Membrane

Low pressure air

Fig. 3.132 *The fluidisation tank*

4 SYSTEMS AND CONTROL

A system is a group of components (parts) that work together to perform a task. In this chapter we will look at systems based on mechanisms, pneumatics, electronics and structures. It is not always necessary to know how each part of a system works in order for you to assemble the system and be able to use it. However, it does help if you understand what is happening so you can add to or improve the system to make things work better, and for those occasions when things go wrong.

Fig. 4.1

A bicycle is a good example of a system. It has a frame, wheels, pedals, gears, brakes and lights. These things together make up a bicycle, they can be regarded as parts within the 'bicycle system'. If you look a little closer (Fig. 4.1) you will see that the frame and the wheels are themselves structural systems with individual parts working together. The pedals, gears and brakes are mechanical systems – the lights are, of course, an electrical system. These smaller systems that contribute to the whole are called **sub-systems**.

Input effort to the pedals	→	Process the bicycle system	→	Output movement

Fig. 4.2 *System block diagram*

Systems can be drawn and are sometimes shown as 'block diagrams' which show an **input**, often in the form of energy, going through a **process** within the system in order to produce a desired **output**. For example on a bicycle the effort of pushing down on the pedals is converted into forward movement by the bicycle. Fig. 4.2 shows this in the form of a block diagram. But this is a system out of control! It needs control – somebody to steer it to make it travel in the right direction. Compare Fig. 4.2 with Fig. 4.3. Fig. 4.3 has **feedback** now which provides the **control.**

Input effort to the pedals	→	Process the bicycle system	→	Output movement in the chosen direction

Feedback
the cyclist
balancing
and steering

Fig. 4.3 *System with feedback control loop*

Control doesn't always have to be provided by a person. In previous chapters computers have been used to control plotters, cutters and machine tools. In a heating system, control is often provided through a thermostat which is an example of electronic control. A thermostat is a device that provides feedback by telling the heating boiler that the room is hot enough and it can stop providing more heat. A thermostatically-controlled heating system saves valuable energy resources and reduces running costs. Fig. 4.4 shows how a heating system can be represented in the form of a block diagram.

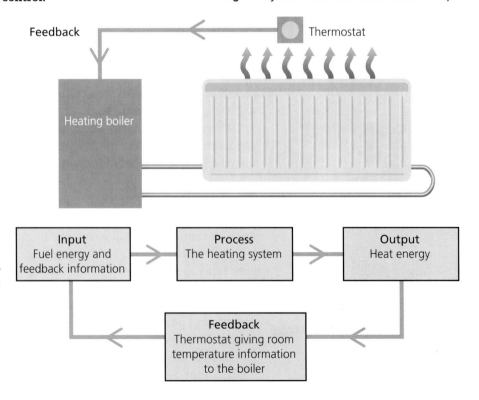

Feedback   Thermostat

Heating boiler

Input Fuel energy and feedback information	→	Process The heating system	→	Output Heat energy

Feedback
Thermostat giving room
temperature information
to the boiler

Fig. 4.4

Mechanical systems

Mechanical systems are systems that use mainly mechanisms. All mechanisms have moving parts and they are designed to do a particular job. Mechanical systems always involve movement and energy.

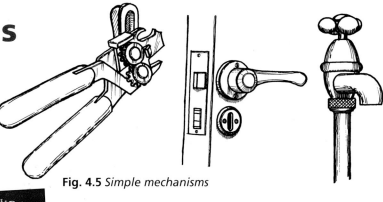

Fig. 4.5 *Simple mechanisms*

Think how many mechanisms you have used today. Water taps, can openers and door handles are all examples of simple mechanisms that you can look at, disassemble and investigate. There are also some very complex mechanisms such as washing machines, sewing machines, lawn mowers and cars. These are all examples of **mechanical systems**. They are made up of many simpler mechanisms called **sub-systems** and they all work together.

Fig. 4.6 *Complex mechanical systems*

Design and Technology is about designing and making products. When the products that you design need a mechanical system in order to function, it is important that you are able to understand how the mechanisms work, and how they contribute to the system that you need. If your bicycle does not stop you soon realise that there may be a problem with the brakes. This is because you have an understanding of how a bicycle works, and you know that it is no good looking at the pedals or the steering to find the fault.

Mechanical advantage ➡

Mechanisms are always designed so that people gain some advantage from using them. They enable you to do something that you could not otherwise do because it would be too hard or too slow. A vice enables you to grip tighter than you could with your hands (Fig. 4.7) and a bicycle enables you to get from one place to another quicker than you could by walking. Both mechanical systems give you an advantage. This is called **mechanical advantage**.

The mechanical advantage (MA) of a system can be given a value. If the effort that you put into a mechanism results in an output that is greater; then the value of the MA will be greater than 1. In a vice for example you might apply a force of 10 Newtons (10 N) and be able to grip something with a force of 80 Newtons (80 N), the MA will be 8, this is calculated by dividing the output (80 N) by the input (10 N)

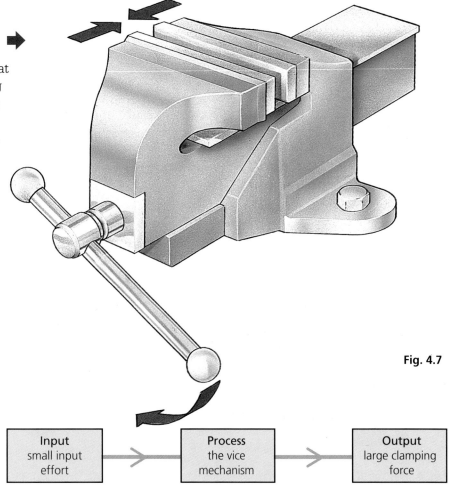

Fig. 4.7

Input		Process		Output
small input effort		the vice mechanism		large clamping force

Types of motion ➡

When an object moves it is said to be in motion. The type of motion is described by the direction in which the object moves. Mechanical systems involve four types of motion:

Rotary motion means the object goes round, like wheels and clock hands.

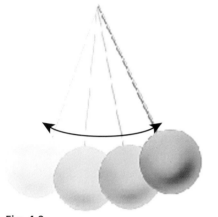

Fig. 4.9

Oscillating motion means the object swings backwards and forwards, like a grandfather clock's pendulum (Fig. 4.9).

Reciprocating motion means the object goes backwards and forwards (or up and down) in a straight line, like a sewing machine needle (Fig. 4.10).

Linear motion means the object moves in a straight line, like a paper trimmer.

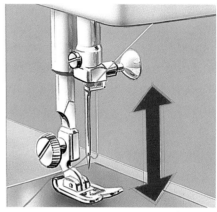

Fig. 4.10

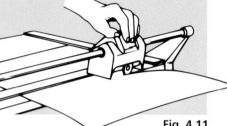

Fig. 4.11

⬅ Mechanisms that bring about change

One of the main functions of mechanical systems is to change motion from one type to another, that is, to change its direction. With a bicycle, for instance, the input motion is rotary, as it turns the pedals round. The output motion, however, is linear as it moves the bicycle in a straight line. A simple device, like a key in a lock, is also a mechanism for changing rotary motion to linear motion.

Fig. 4.12 *A key in a lock and a bicycle change rotary motion to linear motion*

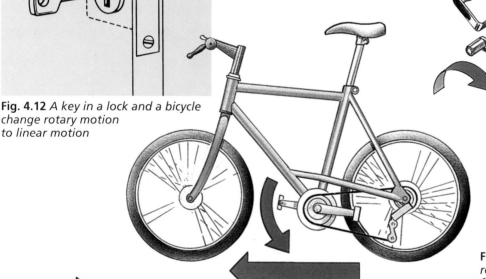

Fig. 4.14 *A hand whisk transfers rotary motion in one plane into faster rotary motion in another*

Look around your school workshops or your kitchen at home and see how many mechanisms you can find that change and transfer motion.

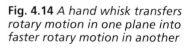

Fig. 4.13 *A spiral ratchet screwdriver changes linear motion to rotary motion*

Levers

The simplest and one of the earliest mechanisms used was the lever. It consists of a rigid bar with a fixed point on which the bar turns. This fixed point is called a pivot. The input is usually called the effort and the output is the movement of the load (see Fig. 4.15). A small amount of effort can be used to move a large load.

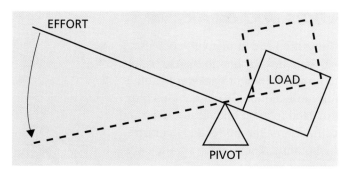

Fig. 4.15

How can such a simple mechanism gain so much mechanical advantage? The advantage is gained by not having the pivot in the middle of the lever. The effort must move the lever further than the distance that the load is moved. What the lever gains in its ability to lift, it loses in the distance that the handle of the lever has to move.

Fig. 4.16 *Everyday levers*

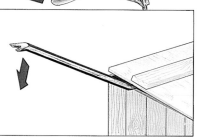

Balance and equilibrium ➡

Balance scales and see-saws are types of levers. They work by balancing one force against another. When balance is achieved, the scales or see-saw are said to be in **equilibrium**.

On a see-saw two teenagers that weigh the same balance each other because the pivot is in the middle and there is no mechanical advantage. A heavy and a light teenager can also balance, but only if the heavy teenager sits nearer to the pivot. If the heavy teenager is twice the weight of the light teenager then the light teenager must sit twice as far from the pivot (see Fig. 4.17).

Fig. 4.17

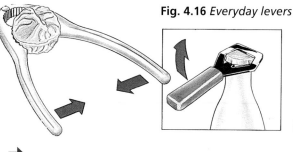

Fig. 4.18 *A simple linkage* **Fig. 4.19** *A bell crank linkage*

⬅ Linkages

Linkages are made by connecting levers together. They are used to link together parts of mechanical systems. They can transfer forces and bring about changes in the direction of forces.

The simple linkage in Fig. 4.18 can be used to reverse the direction of a force, for example, changing a pushing force into a pulling force. The linkage in Fig. 4.19 is used to transfer a force through 90°. This linkage is called a bell crank because it is like an old-fashioned door bell mechanism. It is also the mechanism that operates a bicycle brake (see Fig. 4.20).

The pivot point of a linkage can be positioned to gain mechanical advantage, in the same way as with a lever. If the pivot is not in the middle of the link, then one side of the link must move a further distance than the other (see Fig. 4.21). A small input force can produce a larger output force (over a shorter distance), or a small input movement can produce a larger output movement (with less force). But, as with levers, you can't have it both ways.

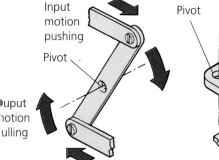
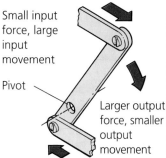

Fig. 4.21 *A linkage with mechanical advantage*

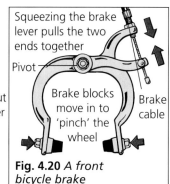

Fig. 4.20 *A front bicycle brake*

Cams and cranks →

Cams are used in many reciprocating mechanisms to change rotary motion to up and down, or backwards and forwards motion. In car engines they are used to open and close valves and contact breaker points and operate fuel pumps. There are several different types of cam, but those which are most useful in design and technology are **rotary cams**.

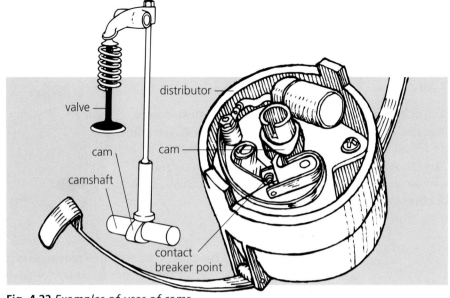

Fig. 4.22 *Examples of uses of cams*

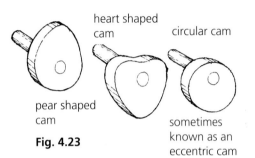

Fig. 4.23

Rotary cams are often made from hardened steel to reduce wear, but they can also be made from acrylic or wood. They are specially shaped, like a pear or heart, or they can be circular with an 'off-centre' hole (see Fig. 4.23). Cams are fitted to a rotating shaft and have a **follower**, which rests on it and moves up and down as the shaft rotates see Fig. 4.24. The different shapes of the cam causes the follower to move in different ways.

Cranks can be used to provide a mechanical advantage using the 'wheel and axle principle' *where a large weight can be lifted with a smaller force.* They are rotary-to-rotary mechanisms also used to gain a large rotational output from a smaller rotational input. One example of this is in a child's tricycle or a 'pop-up' pull along toy where the cranked axle provides reciprocating motion (see Fig. 4.25).

Fig. 4.24

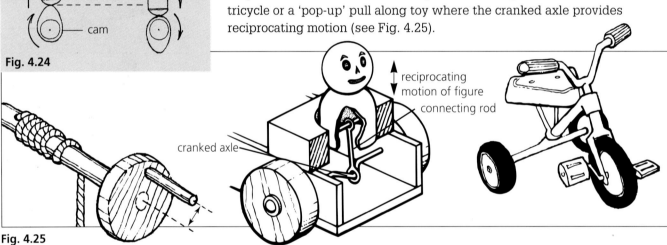

Fig. 4.25

← Inclined planes

Inclined planes, such as slopes and ramps, were used in ancient times to lift huge stone blocks when building large structures like the great pyramids (Fig. 4.26). Mechanical advantage is gained because it is easier to pull a long way up a gentle slope than it is to lift a small vertical distance.

Fig. 4.26

Screws

Screws and bolts are inclined planes wrapped around a cylinder (Fig. 4.27). When a screw is cutting and pulling its way into wood a lot of work is being done. It is the screw's mechanical advantage that enables it to be turned relatively easily.

Screw-based mechanisms such as car jacks (Fig. 4.28) also have a large mechanical advantage, which enables a person to lift a car with little effort.

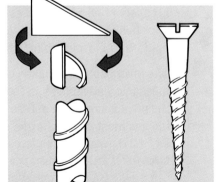

Fig. 4.28

Fig. 4.27

Pulleys

Pulleys for changing and transferring motion

Pulley systems, using pulleys fixed on shafts, are used to transfer rotary motion from one place to another. They can also be used to change the speed of the motion. Pulleys must always fit tightly onto their drive shafts otherwise they will slip and effort and energy will be lost. The speed of rotation is affected by the difference in size between the driver pulley and the driven pulley. If the driver pulley is larger than the driven pulley, then the output speed will be greater than the input speed (see Fig. 4.29). If the driver pulley is smaller than the driven pulley then the output speed will be slower than the input speed (see Fig. 4.30). When pulleys of different sizes are fixed onto the same shaft (stepped pulleys) the speed can be changed by moving the belt from one pulley to another (see Fig. 4.31).

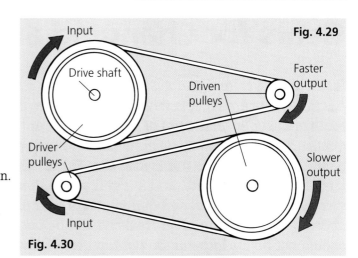

Fig. 4.29

Fig. 4.30

> When you are investigating mechanisms, make sure you never operate any machines with the covers open or removed. ⚠

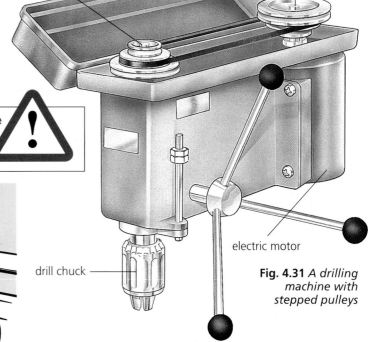

Fig. 4.31 *A drilling machine with stepped pulleys*

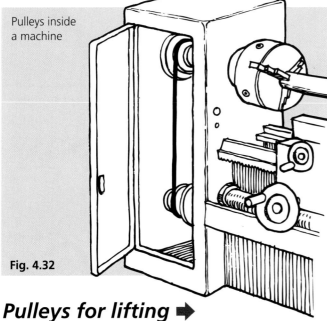

Fig. 4.32

Pulleys for lifting ➡

Free-running pulley systems are often used in warehouses and factories to help lift heavy weights, such as crates and machinery. A two-pulley system like the one shown in Fig. 4.33 has a mechanical advantage of 2. This means that a load can be lifted using half the input effort. But the effort, of course, needs to travel twice the distance.

You can see how this works in the following equation:

Effort × distance moved by effort = Load × distance moved by load

$$2 \times 2 = 4 \times 1$$
$$4 = 4$$

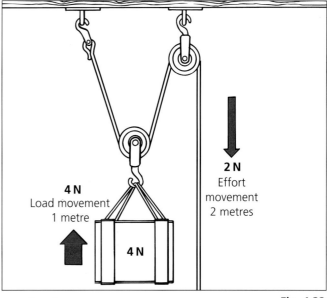

Fig. 4.33

Gears for Changing and Transferring Motion

Like pulley systems, gear systems are used to change and transfer rotary motion. Gears are wheels with teeth which are an equal distance apart. The teeth are usually on the rim of the wheel but are sometimes on the face. Most gears are made from plastic or metal, but in the past and in other cultures gears have been made from wood (see Fig. 4.34). Gear teeth are a special shape called an involute, and it is this shape that helps gears to run together smoothly and to transfer motion from one gear to the next. A system of gears is known as a gear train. Gear trains should be put together with care. They should not be too loose or too tight, otherwise energy may be wasted.

Gears can be used to change speed and to change direction. The input gear to any system is called the driver gear and the output gear is called the driven gear. In a simple (in-line) gear train, as in Fig. 4.35, the gears fitted between the driver and driven gears are called idler gears. They change the direction of rotation. A change in speed within a gear train is achieved by putting together gears with different numbers of teeth. If a driver gear with 40 teeth is driving a driven gear that has 20 teeth, the speed will be double. For every turn of the driver gear the driven gear will turn twice. The number of turns of one gear to

Fig. 4.34 *An old wooden gear system in a windmill*

another is called the gear ratio. The gear ratio for this gear train is 1:2 (one to two). If the driver gear has 20 teeth and the driven gear 40 teeth the gear chain will slow down. For every two turns of the driver gear the driven gear will turn once and will therefore have a gear ratio of 2:1. The number and size of idler gears between the driver and driven gear has no effect upon the gear ratio – they only change the direction.

Driver gear   Driven gear

Idler gear

Fig. 4.35 *Simple gear trains*

Driver gear
40 teeth

Driver gear
20 teeth

Idler gear

Driver gear

30 teeth

Idler gear

Idler gear

Driven gear

Driven gear
20 teeth
Ratio 1:2

Driven gear
40 teeth
Ratio 2:1

Driven gear
20 teeth
Ratio 2:3

Fig. 4.36 *Gear ratios*

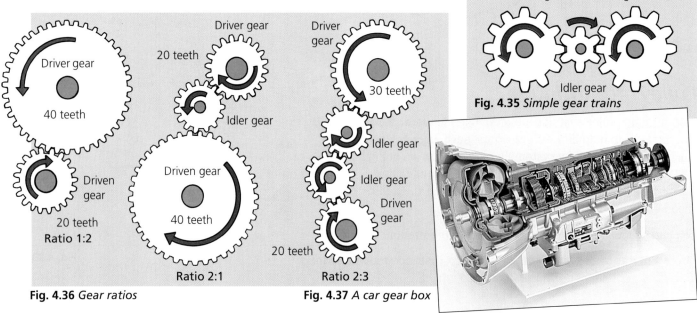

Fig. 4.37 *A car gear box*

Fig. 4.39 *A hand drill*

Bevel gears

Bevel gears are used in pairs to change the angle of rotation through 90° (see Fig. 4.38). Hand drills use bevel gears to both change the direction of rotation and to make the drill rotate fast.

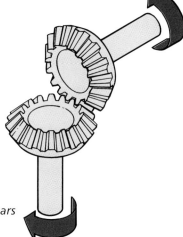

Fig. 4.38 *Bevel gears*

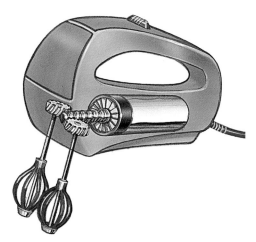

Fig. 4.41 *A worm gear is used to drive the beaters of an electric whisk*

Worm and wormwheel

This is another gear system to change the direction of rotation through 90°. A worm looks like a screw, but it is really a gear with only one long tooth (see Fig. 4.40). This single tooth is wrapped around a cylinder and is used to turn a gear. The gear ratio of worm drives is very low. They are often used to change the high speed of electric motors into more useful speeds.

Worm gear

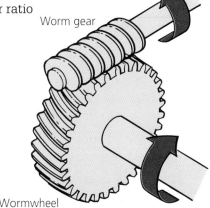

Wormwheel

Fig. 4.40 *Worm and wormwheel*

Rack and pinion ⬇

Rack and pinions change motion from rotary to linear.

A rack is like a flattened out gear wheel. The gear that it works with is called a pinion (see Fig. 4.43). They are used on canal lock gates and in car steering systems.

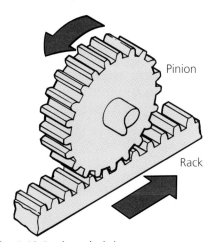

Pinion

Rack

Fig. 4.43 *Rack and pinion*

Fig. 4.42 *A canal lock gate*

Investigate a hand drill from your school workshop. Count the teeth and calculate the ratio.

Mechanical efficiency

An efficient mechanism is one that loses very little energy in doing its job. A loss of energy could mean a loss of money or a waste of resources. Cars, for example, are very inefficient mechanical systems. Only a small percentage of the potential energy of fuel is converted by the car into movement. Most of the energy is lost in the form of friction, mechanical wear, heat, sound and exhaust fumes. Simple lever systems, like the see-saw, are very efficient. This means that most of the effort is converted to work done by the mechanism, and very little energy is lost within the system.

Fig. 4.44 *A car being tuned to improve its mechanical efficiency*

Fig. 4.45

No matter how simple a mechanical system is, to be efficient it needs to be made with care. Its parts need to be clean and smooth, and they must fit together well and not be too loose. Often a drop of oil for lubrication will help. You may have noticed that a rusty bicycle that needs oiling is harder to pedal than one that has been well looked after (Fig. 4.45).

Check out your mechanisms

1 Investigate the mechanisms in your school workshop or your kitchen at home and see how many mechanisms you can find that change and transfer motion. Make a list of those that change the type of motion and a list of those that change the speed of motion. Some things may appear on both lists.

2 Use Meccano or card and paper rivets to model the mechanisms of a bicycle brake and of a tool box.

3 If a driver pulley has a diameter of 60 millimetres, what size must the driven pulley be to make it rotate twice as fast? Check out your answer by modelling the pulley system.

Fig. 4.46 *A mechanism built using Lego*

4 Using modelling kits investigate the gear trains in Fig. 4.36 on page 76. What effect do the idler gears have? What applications can you think of where two idler gears would be useful?

5 Model a gear system that has a 1:4 ratio and does not change direction.

6 Young children often enjoy pull-along toys. Can you think of some ways of adding extra interest to a pull-along toy such as a mechanism that makes part of the toy pop up and down, squeak, flash a light, spin round or wobble about. Design an interesting toy and model the mechanisms using card or a kit.

Fig. 4.47 *A mechanism built using Polymech*

Pneumatic Systems

When air is compressed it stores the energy that was used to compress it. Pneumatic systems use that energy to do work and to make things happen.

Doors on buses and trains, fairground rides and brakes on lorries all use pneumatic systems. You may have heard them hiss as the compressed air that has done its work is allowed to escape. You may have experienced pneumatic drills at the dentist and much larger ones digging up the road. Pneumatic systems are very common and are used a lot in the manufacturing industry to move things about, clamp them down, and to power hand tools like drills and screwdrivers.

The principles are quite straightforward. You need some way of compressing air, somewhere to store it, and then you can use it. Compressors are like pumps and are usually driven by electric motors. The air is sucked in through filters to make it clean and it is then forced into a large tank called a receiver. Compressed air from the receiver goes through a pressure regulator and, using plastic or metal pipes, is connected to a pneumatic system.

Fig. 4.48 *The energy that a pneumatic road drill uses is energy that is stored when the air is compressed*

Component Symbols

Once you understand the symbols used to represent pneumatic components it is easy to work out what they do. The basic parts of most conventional pneumatic systems are valves to control the flow of air, and cylinders to provide straight line movement.

In the example shown below the cylinder operates when the valve is pressed. The valve is a three-port valve (3PV). Port 1 is connected to the air supply, port 2 is connected to the cylinder and port 3 is open to act as an exhaust. Pneumatic systems are usually shown in schematic form. Fig. 4.50 shows a schematic diagram and Fig. 4.49 shows the actual components of a pneumatic system.

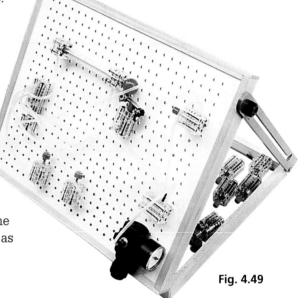

Fig. 4.49

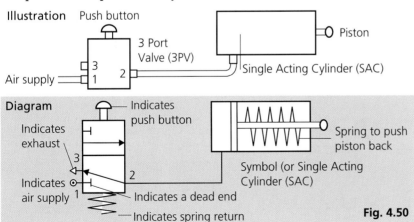

Fig. 4.50

The symbol for the single-acting cylinder (SAC); is easy to understand, air pushes the piston out and when the air is exhausted the spring pushes the piston back.

The symbol for the 3PV is less clear because it is shown in two halves. The top half shows the connections in the valve when the button is operated and the bottom half shows the connections when the button is not operated (at rest). Fig. 4.51 explains this in more detail.

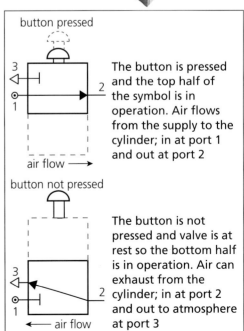

button pressed

The button is pressed and the top half of the symbol is in operation. Air flows from the supply to the cylinder; in at port 1 and out at port 2

air flow →

button not pressed

The button is not pressed and valve is at rest so the bottom half is in operation. Air can exhaust from the cylinder; in at port 2 and out to atmosphere at port 3

← air flow

Fig. 4.51 *The operation of a 3 port valve (3PV)*

Basic pneumatic control circuits

You can see here some pneumatic circuits that are often sub-systems within circuits used to operate and control a whole range of devices in real situations. All of these circuits can be modelled using low pressure pneumatics which are safe and quick in school situations. The best way to learn about pneumatics is to study the circuits and try to model them.

First here are some simple safety guidelines when using pneumatic systems.
Never blow compressed air at anyone.
Connect up all components before switching on the air supply.
Keep your hands out of the way of moving parts, mainly pistons.
Route air lines so that people do not trip over them.

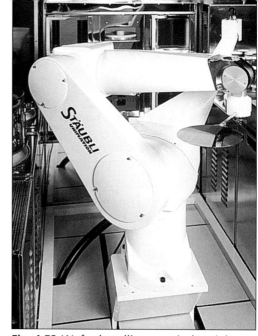

Fig. 4.52 *Wafer handling – an industrial process that uses pneumatic control*

An AND circuit

In the illustration (Fig. 4.53) you can see an application of an AND circuit – a manufacturing process that has to be guarded for safety. The process shown uses a pneumatic cylinder to blank out thin sheet steel for badges. The operation is **interlocked** to the safety guard so that it is not possible for the operator's hand to be inside the guard when it operates. This is done by ensuring that if the guard is not in place the operator's process switch will not work. The operation needs to be switched by the operator **AND** the guard.

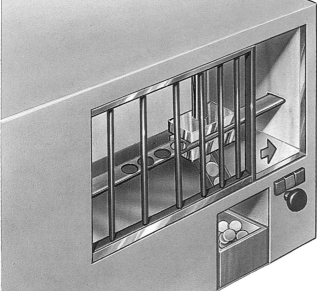

Fig. 4.53 *Guarded pneumatic industrial process*

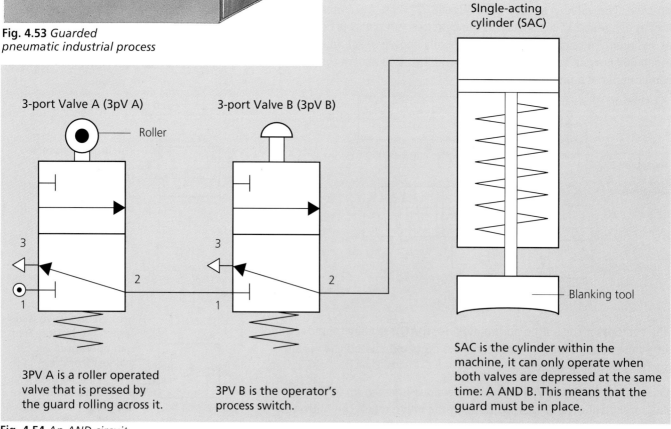

3-port Valve A (3pV A) — Roller

3-port Valve B (3pV B)

SIngle-acting cylinder (SAC)

Blanking tool

3PV A is a roller operated valve that is pressed by the guard rolling across it.

3PV B is the operator's process switch.

SAC is the cylinder within the machine, it can only operate when both valves are depressed at the same time: A AND B. This means that the guard must be in place.

Fig. 4.54 *An AND circuit*

An OR circuit

OR circuits, like the one shown in Figs. 4.55 and 4.56 operate if **either** of the valves are pressed. 3PV C **OR** 3PV D. This circuit requires one extra component; a **shuttle valve.** Look at the circuit, it is intended that either valve operates the cylinder but if a simple 'T' connection was used in place of the shuttle valve then as either valve was pressed the air would exhaust through the other one.

The shuttle valve is simply a ball in a tube that blocks off the opposite port so that the air goes to the cylinder (see Fig. 4.57).

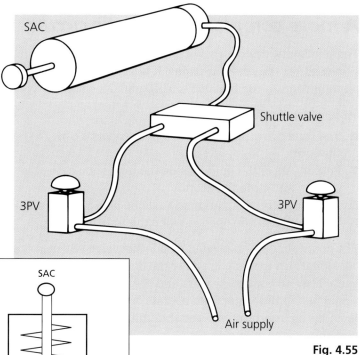

Fig. 4.55

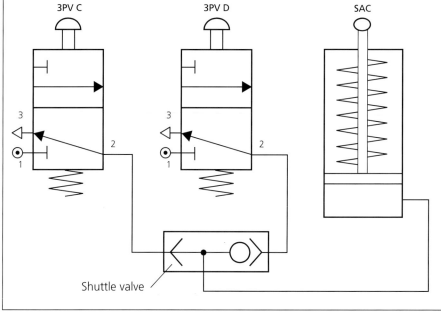

Fig. 4.56 *An OR Circuit*

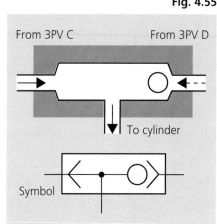

Fig. 4.57 *Shuttle valve*

← *Double-acting cylinders*

The circuit shown here (Fig. 4.58) introduces three new components, **5-port valves** (5PV), **double-acting cylinders** (DAC) and a **flow control valve**. Double-acting cylinders have no spring to make them return so they need to be pushed in both directions. The 5-port valve has no spring either so it can be operated by pushing on either end. 5-port valves can also be air operated.

In the circuit the air supply is connected to port 1. Push button 'A' switches the supply to port 4 to send the piston out (positive) and push button 'B' switches the supply to port 2 to send the piston in (negative).

The function of a flow control valve is to slow down the action of the cylinder by restricting the outgoing (exhausting) air flow. This piston goes positive at a controlled speed and negative fast.

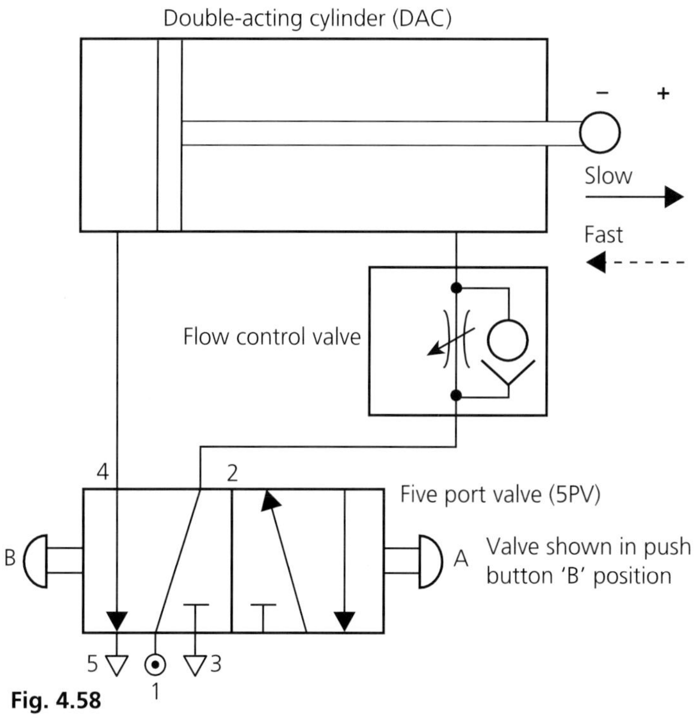

Fig. 4.58

A more complex pneumatic circuit

The pneumatic system shown here pieces together the sub-systems from the previous pages. It is the type of circuit used on train doors, a combination of AND and OR circuits.

System specification:

■ The train driver should be able to open and close the doors.

■ Passengers or the guard inside the train should be able to open and close the doors.

■ Passengers on the platform should be able to open the doors.

■ The doors can't be opened when the train is moving.

The door cylinder is activated by a 5-port valve which is operated by an 'air signal'. Up to this point all of the lines can be regarded as signal lines. They do not do any work and are shown as dashed lines. The signal part of the system can operate at a low pressure and the 5PV provides an **interface** between the signal and the high pressure operation of the door cylinder.

Fig. 4.59 *Intercity train*

Fig. 4.60 *Train door push-buttons*

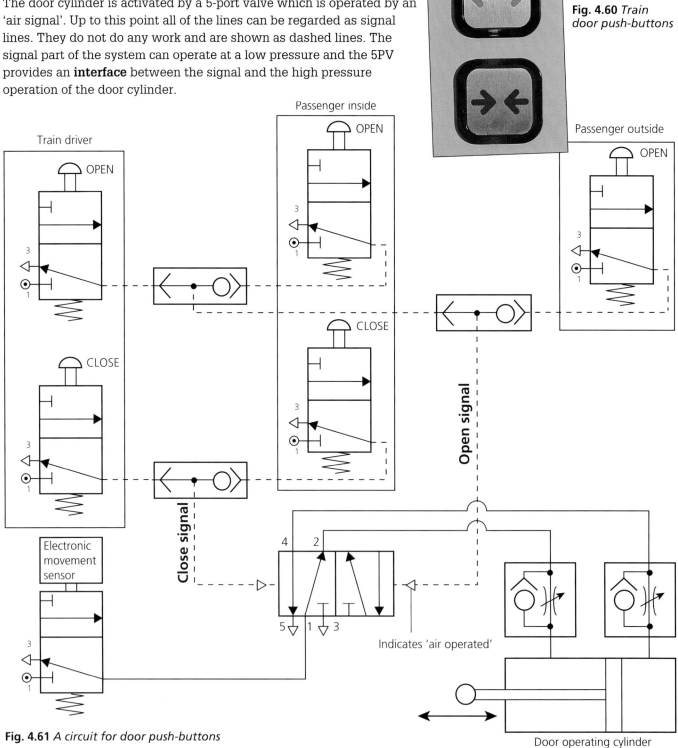

Fig. 4.61 *A circuit for door push-buttons*

Alternative pneumatics – the 'shadow' air muscle

The 'shadow' air muscle is a device developed by a group of people working on a project to build a domestic robot. The air muscle works like a human muscle and can be used to make things move using short linear contractions, just like the muscles in your arms and legs.

The muscle is very simply a short length of rubber tube with some braiding over it. The ends of the braiding are formed into loops so that they can be used to attach things and the tube is sealed and attached to an air supply. When low pressure air is supplied the tube expands causing the muscle to shorten.

Fig. 4.62 *The shadow air muscle*

Fig. 4.63 *System using pump and pop bottle*

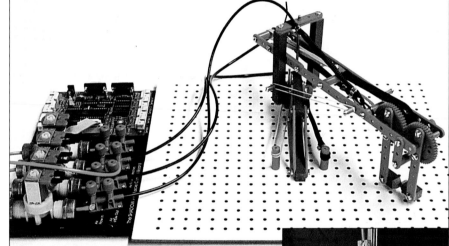

Fig. 4.64 *An air muscle connected to a demonstration rig*

The air pressure required is low so a simple 'pump and pop bottle' arrangement like that shown in Fig. 4.63 can be used. This arrangement can also be used with conventional low pressure pneumatic systems.

- Never use glass bottles.
- Never connect bottles to an air compressor.

Check out your pneumatics

1 Make a list of as many examples of the everyday use of pneumatic systems as you can, and don't forget aerosols and beer-can 'widgets'.

2 Draw a pneumatic AND circuit that uses three 3-port valves to control a single acting cylinder.

3 Draw a pneumatic OR circuit and explain why it is necessary to use a shuttle valve.

4 Explain in simple short steps how the 5-port valve in Fig. 4.61 operates within the train door opening and closing circuit.

5 Design a pneumatic car-park barrier. You can use either conventional pneumatics or air muscles. You may need to refer to the earlier section on mechanical systems.

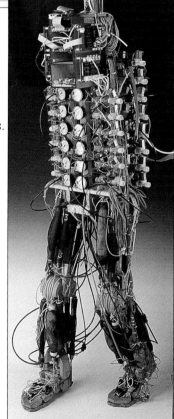

Fig. 4.65 *The shadow robot uses computer controlled low pressure pneumatics and air muscles*

Electronic systems

Electronic systems are all around us. Look at the electrical appliances in many homes – the refrigerator, the washing machine, the microwave oven, the television and the video recorder. These all use electricity to do their work and they are all controlled by miniature electronic systems. Even gas, and oil-fired heating systems at home or at school are controlled by electronic systems.

Fig. 4.66 *Electronic systems are all around us*

Electrical energy

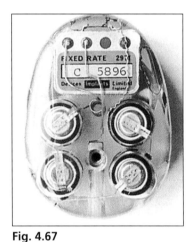

Fig. 4.67

Some electrical appliances, particularly those that produce heat, such as kettles and cookers, use a lot of energy. Electronic systems, however, use very little energy and for this reason they can be run on the electrical energy stored on batteries. Fig. 4.67 shows a 'pacemaker'. This is a device that people with heart problems have fitted into their chests in order to keep their heartbeat regular. You can clearly see the small batteries that will keep the device operating for many years. These are Nycam batteries, similar to those used in watches. Batteries are sometimes chosen because of their physical size but they are also chosen to suit the **voltage** requirements of the device that they will power. The drive motor in most personal stereos requires 3 volts so it is necessary to use two 1.5 volt batteries. Have a look in your personal stereo or calculator and see what voltage it requires.

Voltage, which is measured in **volts**, is the driving force for the flow of electrical **current**. Electrical current is measured in **amps** (amperes). Current does the work in electrical systems and the more current that a device needs, the quicker the battery will be exhausted or 'run down'.

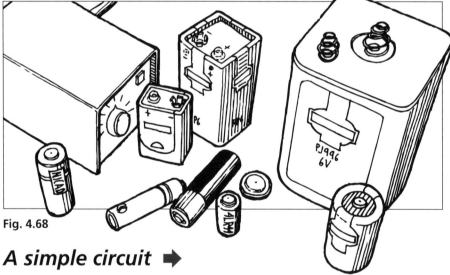

Fig. 4.68

A simple circuit ➡

Fig. 4.69 shows a simple **circuit** to switch on and off a light bulb. The circuit contains a bulb, a switch, a battery and, of course, a battery connector and some wire. They are joined together to form the circuit which is like a running track; it provides a complete route around which the electricity can flow.

If the circuit is broken at any point then electricity will not flow and, in this case, the bulb will not light up. The function of the switch in a circuit is to make a break that can be connected and disconnected at will. Fig. 4.70 shows the simple circuit in the form of a **circuit diagram**. Whenever a circuit diagram is drawn internationally agreed symbols are always used to represent the components and the wire is drawn as straight lines.

Bulb

Switch

Symbol for battery

Fig. 4.70

Fig. 4.69

Some basic electronic components

Switches

Switches are included in circuits to 'make' or 'break' connections. Fig. 4.71 shows some of the types available.

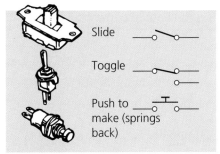

Slide

Toggle

Push to make (springs back)

Fig. 4.71

Resistors

Resistors resist and direct the flow of electricity. There are two basic types: fixed and variable. Fixed resistors have a fixed resistance which is indicated by a colour code. Resistance is measured in ohms, the symbol for which is W. The resistor colour codes are shown in Fig. 4.82.

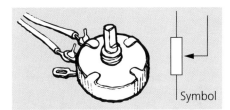

Symbol

Fig. 4.72 *A fixed resistor*

The resistance of a variable resistor can be changed by turning its spindle. You can set the resistance from zero up to the value given on the base of the component (e.g. 10 kW).

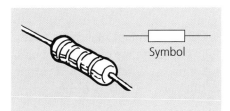

Symbol

Fig. 4.73 *A variable resistor*

A preset is a very small variable resistor. It can be adjusted using a small screwdriver.

Screwdriver slot

Symbol

Fig. 4.74 *A preset resistor*

Sensors

A light dependent resistor (LDR) senses light and changes its resistance as the light intensity changes. It's resistance is *high* in the *dark* and *low* in *bright light*.

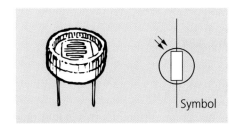

Symbol

Fig. 4.75 *Light sensor*

A thermistor senses heat and reacts to temperature changes. It has a *high* resistance when it is *cold*, and a *low* resistance when it is *hot*.

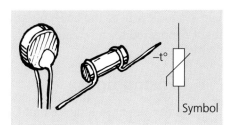

–t°

Symbol

Fig. 4.76 *Temperature sensor*

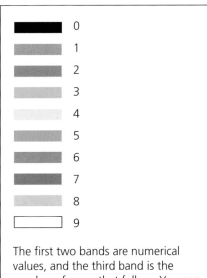

0
1
2
3
4
5
6
7
8
9

The first two bands are numerical values, and the third band is the number of zeros that follow. You can ignore the silver or gold band.

Orange | Orange | Brown | Gold or
3 | 3 | 0 | silver

This gives 330 ohms

Fig. 4.82 *Resistor colour codes*

Output devices (transducers)

Bulbs can be connected either way round.

Holder

Symbol

Fig. 4.77 *Bulb*

LEDs (Light emitting diodes) are red, green or amber in colour. They must be connected the right way round and they need a protective resistor.

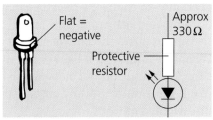

Flat = negative

Approx 330 Ω

Protective resistor

Fig. 4.78 *Light emitting diode*

Buzzers give a continuous sound and make useful alarms.

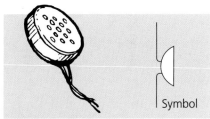

Symbol

Fig. 4.79 *Buzzer*

Speakers can be used to create continuous noises, notes or speech.

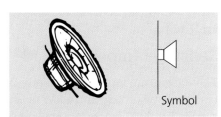

Symbol

Fig. 4.80 *Speaker*

Small DC **motors** can be connected either way round, so running in either direction. They are used to create movement (e.g. in a model car).

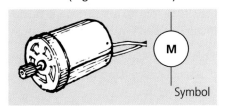

M

Symbol

Fig. 4.81 *Motor*

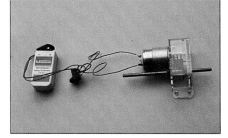

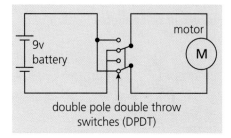

Fig. 4.83

double pole double throw
switches (DPDT)

An interesting motor switching circuit

By using a double-pole, double-throw switch an electric motor can be switched to run in either direction (Fig. 4.83). A double-pole, double-throw switch is like two switches joined together. Electrical current flows from the '+' terminal of a battery to the '−' terminal. Now, look at the circuit diagram in Fig. 4.84 and see how by 'throwing' the switch the flow of current to the motor is reversed. Reversing the flow of current to a motor will change its direction.

Fig. 4.84

Useful transistor circuits

Transistors are process components they act as sensitive electronic switches in the following circuits. You can see in Fig. 4.85 that they have three legs. These must be connected the correct way round for it to work. It is often a good idea to connect a resistor to the 'base' (input), of the transistor to keep it from being damaged. This is called a 'protective' or 'limiting' resistor because it limits the flow of current in order to protect the transistor. When the input at the base of the transistor rises to 0.6 volts the transistor switches on the output side and allows current to flow in at the collector and out at the emitter. So, any output component connected to the collector will be switched on.

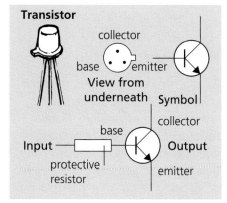

Fig. 4.85

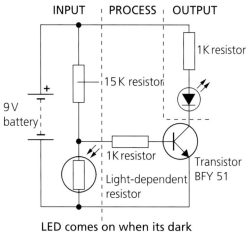

LED comes on when its dark

Fig. 4.86

Sensing light

In the circuit in Figs 4.86 and 4.87 a light-dependent resistor is used as the input. When the light level falls its resistance goes higher and the voltage at the base of the transistor rises, switching it on. Current then flows and the output device, in this case an LED, is turned on.

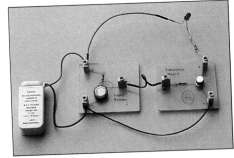

Circuits like this are used to control street lighting, illuminated road signs and safety lighting in shops, factories and offices.

Fig. 4.87

Sensing temperature ➡

Thermistors are input components; they have a high resistance when cold and a low resistance when hot. This circuit (Fig. 4.88) works in a similar way to the light-sensing circuit above. In this case, the thermistor's temperature drops so its resistance increases and the input voltage to the transistor rises and so it switches on. In this case one transistor switches on another transistor which in turn switches on the buzzer. This makes the circuit more sensitive. It is an arrangement called a **darlington pair** and it can be used with most transistor switching circuits.

This type of circuit could provide a warning device for chemical processing plants, greenhouses or cold storage units.

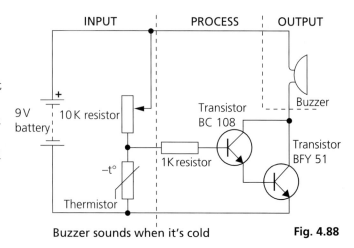

Buzzer sounds when it's cold

Fig. 4.88

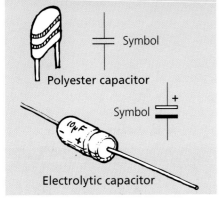

Symbol

Polyester capacitor

Symbol

Electrolytic capacitor

Fig. 4.89 *Electrolytic capacitor*

Timing circuits

A simple time delay circuit can be made using a transistor switch and a **capacitor**. Capacitors are electronic components that are able to store an electrical charge. The amount stored is measured in micro-farads (μF). There are two common types of capacitor: polyester capacitors, which have only small values, and electrolytic capacitors, which are the type to use in timing circuits.

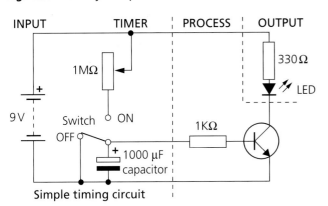

Fig. 4.90

The circuit shown in Fig. 4.90 works like this. When the switch is moved to the ON position electric current flows through the variable resistor into the capacitor and the capacitor starts to 'charge up'. As this happens the voltage across it rises. When the voltage at the base of the transistor reaches 0.6 volts it switches on, switching on the output; in this case an LED.

The reason for having a variable resistor in the circuit is so that you can adjust the length of time before the transistor switches on.

Modelling electronic circuits

It is always a good idea to '**model**' or '**prototype**' an electronic circuit before you go on to manufacture it. Your model will enable you to test the circuit to make sure that it works and it will help you to decide upon the shape and type of case that you may decide to use. There are many ways to model electronic circuits. A very simple method is to use a piece of soft wood with some wood screws and screw cups to grip the wires and hold down the components (see Fig. 4.91).

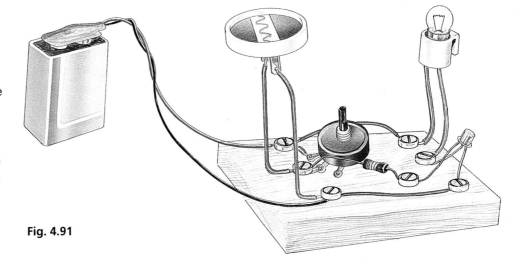

Fig. 4.91

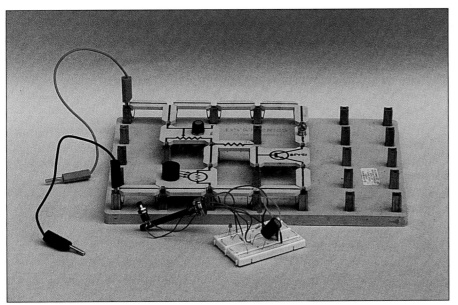

Another method is to use one of the commercially available circuit modelling kits such as 'Locktronics' or you can use 'prototyping board'. You can see both of these methods in the photograph (Fig. 4.92). Prototyping board (breadboard) is rather fiddly but it is better for more complex circuits particularly when using ICs (see page 86).

Fig. 4.92 *A Locktronics system and prototype modelling board*

Building a permanent circuit

The best way to turn your circuit design into a permanent circuit is to make a printed circuit. In any electronic product such as a television set or a personal stereo you will see printed circuit boards or PCBs. Printed circuit board is thin glass-reinforced-plastic board (GRP) coated with a layer of copper. To use the board to connect together electronic components you simply remove unwanted copper with acid to leave behind strips of copper which form the 'wire' for your circuit.

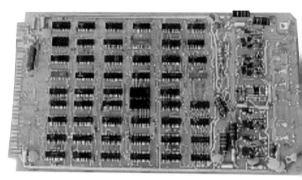

Fig. 4.93 *A printed circuit board*

Making a PCB

Stage 1 – Planning your layout ➡

You can produce a PCB layout by working from your circuit diagram and your circuit prototype. The layout should have the components of the correct size and the component connections in the correct place. Look in particular at the transistor in the layout (Fig. 4.94). You can see that the base connection is not quite the same as it is when represented by a symbol on a circuit diagram; it needs to be the same as the actual component. Try to make your layout as compact as possible and have in mind the product that the circuit board is designed to fit into.

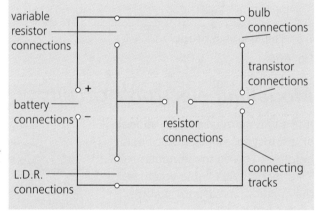

Fig. 4.94

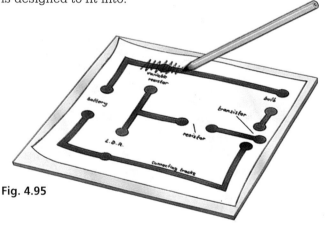

Fig. 4.95

Stage 3 – Etching ➡

Etching with ferric chloride solution, which is a type of acid, removes the copper that is not required in order to form the circuit. This is carried out in a 'bubble etch tank'. If you have used a pencil or tracing to transfer your layout then you need to go over your circuit with an 'etch resist' pen otherwise it will all be eaten away and you will have nothing left.

> You must use tongs to handle your circuit board and wear goggles and gloves. When you have removed your board, wash it thoroughly in water and clean it gently with wire wool.

⬅ Stage 2 – Preparing the PCB

Your circuit layout now needs to be transferred to the copper side of the PCB. This can be done in a number of ways. For most boards you can use rub-down transfers or tracing paper (Fig. 4.95). You need to be very careful at this stage; it is very easy to get the PCB layout the wrong way up. Remember that the components will by fitted to the opposite side of the board from the copper so you need to turn your layout over.

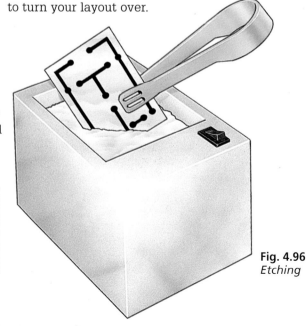

Fig. 4.96
Etching

Stage 4 – Drilling

It is best to use a special PCB drill to make the holes for the legs of your components. The drill needs to be the correct size to suit the components and it needs to rotate very fast. Be sure to support your board on a piece of scrap wood and hold it firmly so that you don't snap the drill (Fig. 4.97).

Fig. 4.97

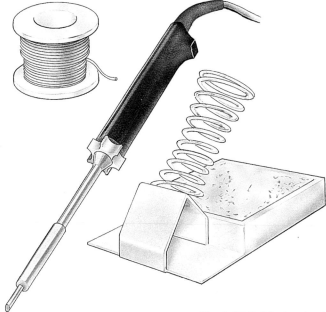

Fig. 4.98 *Soldering tools*

Stage 5 – Soldering ➡

Components and wires are joined to the circuit board using a soldering iron and solder. Solder is a type of metal, an alloy of tin and lead. It melts at a relatively low temperature, around 200°C, and then sets again when the heat is removed.

> When soldering, take care not to breathe in fumes. ⚠

The best solder to use is 'multi-core' solder. This contains a cleaning agent or 'flux' which helps to ensure a good joint. Cleanliness is very important to the success of soldering: try to avoid touching the areas that you are going to solder. Dirt and oils from your skin are the most common cause of poorly soldered joints.

Some components, such as transistors and LED's, can be damaged if they are allowed to get too hot. It is a good idea to use a small pair of pliers to act as a 'heat sink' between the board and the component (Fig. 4.100). This will take away some of the heat as you are soldering.

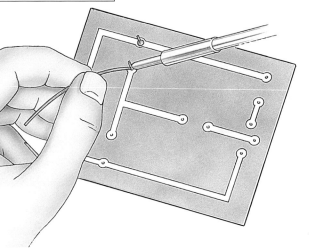

Fig. 4.99 *Soldering*

Six steps to soldering success

1 Clean the board and all components.

2 Make sure that the soldering iron is clean and the tip is coated with a thin layer of solder.

3 Put the component leg through the board and support both the board and component so that your hands are free.

4 Heat the component leg and the copper track with the soldering iron.

5 Apply the solder to the component and not to the iron. The solder will run when the heat is right.

6 Allow your work to cool without moving it about.

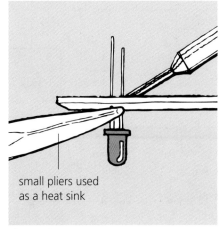

small pliers used as a heat sink

Fig. 4.100

Integrated circuits

Integrated circuits, also known as ICs or chips, are complete electronic circuits that have been miniaturised and etched onto a tiny piece of silicon. The silicon 'chip' (Fig. 4.101) is normally $0.2\,mm^2$, so small that it could pass through the eye of a needle. Circuits this small have to be encased in plastic and have legs added so that electrical connections can be made to them (Fig. 4.102). ICs of various sizes and complexity can be made very cheaply and are found in all possible electronic devices (Fig. 4.103), from watches to computers.

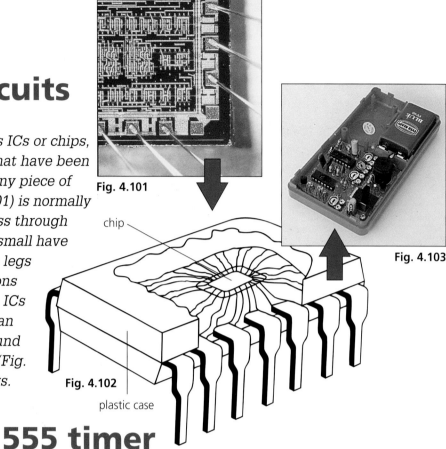

Fig. 4.101

Fig. 4.103

Fig. 4.102

chip

plastic case

555 timer

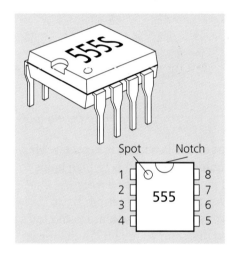

The 555 timer is an '8 pin integrated circuit'. This means that it has 8 'legs'. These are numbered 1 to 8 as shown in Fig. 4.104. The pins are not numbered on the actual IC but pin 1 can be located by reference to the 'spot' or 'notch' in the plastic casing. In circuit diagrams the IC is often shown as a square, and the pin numbers are put on at any convenient place. This is to make the diagram clearer and reduce the number of unconnected lines that have to cross each other.

Fig. 4.104 *Pin numbers on integrated circuits*

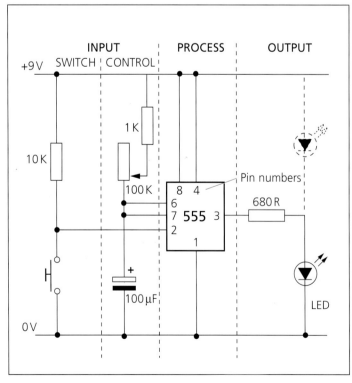

← *A monostable timing circuit*

By using just a few extra components the 555 timer can be used to provide a time period before it turns an output on or off. It can be used for egg timers, game timers or for timing chemical processes such as photographic processing. The circuit in Fig. 4.105 will provide a time period of around 10 seconds.

How it works!

The push button switch signals the start of the timed period and the LED is switched on. At the end of the period the LED goes off. If you put the LED in the position shown by the dotted lines it will be off for the timed period and will then turn on.

It is difficult to be precise about the time but it can be adjusted and calibrated using the variable resistor. A good guide to remember is that $100\,k\Omega$ and $100\,\mu F$ give 10 seconds. Larger values of either resistor or capacitor increase the time period.

Fig. 4.105

Astable timing circuits

The 555 timer can be set up to work in an 'astable mode'. This means that it keeps switching on/off, on/off continuously. This will make lights flash or generate a noise through a loudspeaker. The circuit diagrams in Figs 4.106 and 4.107 show these arrangements.

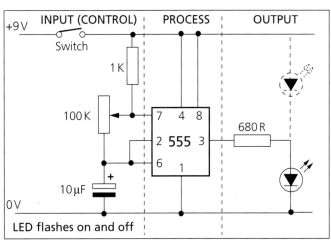

LED flashes on and off

Fig. 4.106

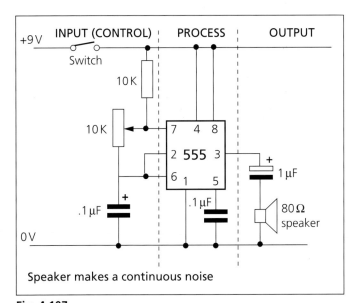

Speaker makes a continuous noise

Fig. 4.107

How it works!

Once the switch is closed the timer starts and the state of the output continuously changes. In Fig. 4.106 adding a second LED in the position shown by the dotted lines will cause them both to flash alternatively. The variable resistor in these circuits enables you to change the rate. In the loudspeaker circuit, Fig. 4.107, the sound can be made to change using the variable resistor so that with some practice you can actually play a tune.

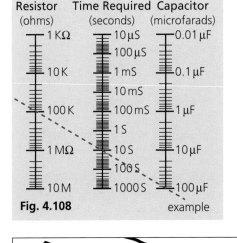

Resistor (ohms)	Time Required (seconds)	Capacitor (microfarads)
1 KΩ	10 µS	0.01 µF
	100 µS	
10 K	1 mS	0.1 µF
	10 mS	
100 K	100 mS	1 µF
	1 S	
1 MΩ	10 S	10 µF
	100 S	
10 M	1000 S	100 µF

Fig. 4.108   example

◀ Timing Guide

The chart in Fig. 4.108 will act as a guide for both monostable and astable circuits for selecting the values of resistors and capacitors to achieve the time that you need.

Check out your electronics

1 List ten electrical or electronic devices from around your home that you think contain integrated circuits.

2 Look at the circuit modelled on page 83 Fig. 4.91. Draw the circuit diagram, explain how the circuit works and suggest what it might be used for.

3 Sometimes it is not easy to tell if a household fuse has blown. Design and circuit that will act as a fuse tester. Layout your circuit design on a PCB that is as small as you can make it. (You will need to find out the size of a fuse).

4 Design a funny face badge that has eyes that light up. Can you design a circuit that will make the eyes flash on and off alternatively?

5 Design a PCB layout for an egg timer circuit using a 555 timer. You will find that graph paper will be useful.

Fig. 4.109 *A printed circuit board*

Microprocessor control

Microprocessors are at the heart of many control systems. At home they can be found in washing machines, in industry they are used in robots and machine tools, even whole manufacturing processes with many machines are sometimes controlled by a microprocessor. A microprocessor is the part of the computer that does all of the work. The input device is usually a keyboard and the output device is usually a monitor screen (VDU), but this does not have to be the case. By using an **interface** the microprocessor can be connected to other forms of input and respond with other forms of output.

Fig. 4.110 *Industrial robots are controlled by microprocessors*

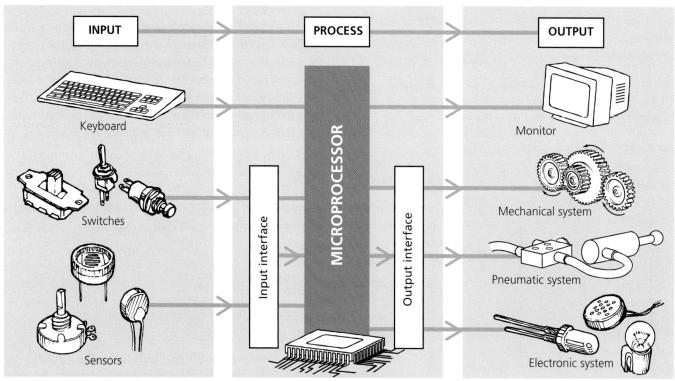

Fig. 4.111 *Microprocessors are at the heart of many control systems*

Programming

Before you can write a program to instruct a computer control system you must know what you want the system to do. It is important to always start by breaking down the sequence that you want the system to follow into small action points. These can then be built into a **flow chart**.

Flow charts use symbols to indicate the nature of the operation being carried out. The three symbols shown below will be enough for most programs.

The boy in Fig. 4.112 is using a computer to control a model of a mechanical system. The interface box provides both the input and the output interfaces. He is using the keyboard and switches on the model to provide input. Electric motors and lights are connected to the output.

Fig. 4.112

Start or stop

Carry out a function

Make a YES or NO decision

A control program example

The flow chart shown in Fig. 4.114 is for a program to control a pedestrian road crossing.

The program starts by turning on the green road light and the red man pedestrian light and then it waits for the button to be pushed by continually checking if this has happened. When the button has been pressed it moves on to the next decision by asking the question 'has the traffic been flowing for a reasonable amount of time?' If not, it waits for that time to elapse. When the specified time has elapsed, the program goes into a **procedure** called 'crossing sequence'. The flow chart for the procedure shown in Fig. 4.115. Procedures are very useful in writing programs – they can be 'called up' at any point, even more than once, and they can be borrowed for other programs.

Study the flow charts carefully. You will notice that although the main program has an end, it can never actually get to it. When the procedure ends it goes back to the beginning of the main program. When creating flow charts for programs it is considered good practice to keep the YES line flowing downwards.

Turning your flow chart into an actual program will depend upon the software that you are using. Some software is structured like a flow chart and can be put together, tried out and modified by moving the flow chart symbols around on the screen (Fig. 4.116). Other software is written, or selected, in the form of statements (Fig. 4.117). Both types have advantages and disadvantages; whichever you use it is important to know beforehand what you are trying to achieve.

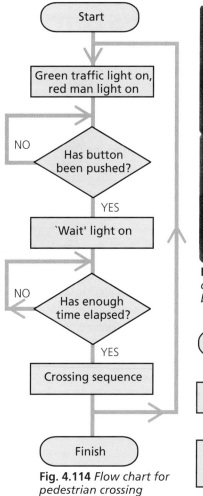

Fig. 4.114 Flow chart for pedestrian crossing

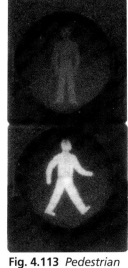

Fig. 4.113 Pedestrian crossing lights, operated by a control program

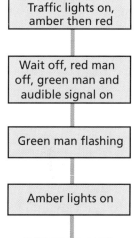

Fig. 4.115 Crossing sequence procedure

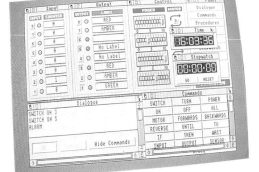

Fig. 4.117 'Coco' software

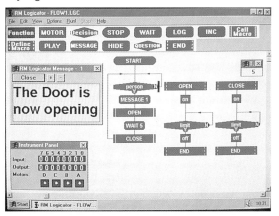

Fig. 4.116 'Logicator' software

Create a flow chart for greenhouse control

The aim is to control the temperature of a greenhouse by monitoring the temperature – opening the window when it is too hot and turning on the heater whe it is too cold. The temperature is sensed by an electronic system, the window is opened by a mechanical system and the heating is provided by an electrical system. In order not to waste energy the greenhouse must be able to have the window closed and the heating off.

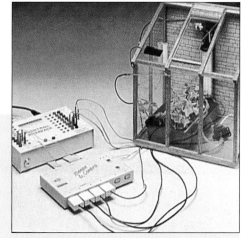

Fig. 4.118 Controlling the temperature of a greenhouse

Structural systems

Many people think that structures are just large constructions, such as tall buildings, bridges and electricity pylons. These are structures, of course, but so are chairs and drinks cans. Structures are things that provide support.

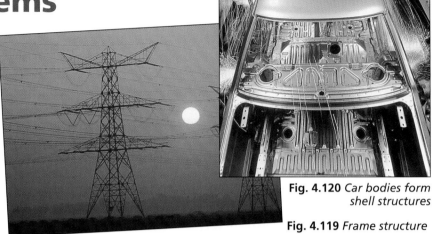

Fig. 4.120 *Car bodies form shell structures*

Fig. 4.119 *Frame structure*

Most structures are really systems, and are made up of parts called **members**. The structural members work together like a team. In some structures, such as those in electricity pylons and climbing frames, it is easy to see the individual members. This is because they are **frame structures**. Some other types of structures, like drinks cans and car bodies, do not have a frame, and these are known as **shell structures**. Look at the two types of sledge in Fig. 4.121. One is a wooden frame structure and the other is a shell structure made from a plastic material known as polypropylene.

Fig. 4.121

Structures are made from different materials, depending upon the job the they have to do. Look at the school chair in Fig. 4.122. It consists of a tubular steel frame structure that supports a polypropylene shell structure that in turn supports the sitter. This chair is a structural system that combines both a frame structure and a shell structure. Tubular steel is chosen because it is strong and light. Polypropylene is used because it is tough, easy to mould and easy to keep clean. These materials are chosen because they have the qualities needed for the making and for the everyday use of a school chair.

Fig. 4.122 *Combined structure*

Structures in nature ➡

Structures are not new. Nature produced the first structures millions of years ago and has been developing them ever since. Egg shells, designed to contain and protect their contents, existed long before drinks cans and car bodies. A spider's web is an extremely strong structure in terms of the weight it will support. You can also think of your body as a complex structural system. Your skeleton provides most of the rigid support for your body, and anchorage for your muscles. It also provides protection and support for delicate and flexible structures, such as your heart and lungs.

Fig. 4.123 *A strong natural structure*

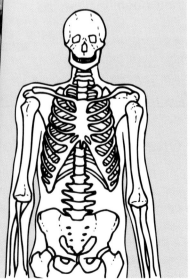

Fig. 4.124

Forces

Structures are designed to withstand forces acting upon them, but sometimes structures collapse or break down. This is called **structural failure**. For example, bridges are designed to carry the weight of traffic or trains crossing them. If a bridge collapses, a terrible accident could occur. Fig. 4.125 shows a picture of the Tay Railway Bridge when it collapsed in 1879.

Chairs are designed for people to sit on, and although they can be made for use by even the heaviest person, they sometimes collapse if a person rocks about, or swings back on them (Fig. 4.126). This is because a chair has been designed to support a **static force**, like that applied by somebody sitting still on it. Chairs are not really designed for **dynamic forces**. Dynamic forces are forces that suddenly change.

There are different kinds of forces. Some forces tend to squash structures, like the force that acts on chair legs when somebody sits on a chair. This is called **compression**. Other forces pull – for example, a rope when it is used to tow a car. This is called **tension**. Sometimes forces combine to **bend** and **twist** structures (see Fig. 4.127).

Structures often have to be designed to withstand different types of forces, and combinations of forces, that can be both static and dynamic. Think of the changing combinations of forces that an aeroplane has to withstand when it takes off, flies through high winds and thunderstorms, and lands.

Fig. **4.125**

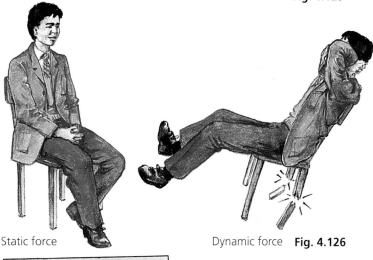

Static force   Dynamic force   Fig. **4.126**

Bending

Twisting

JAM

Tension

Compression   Fig. **4.127**

Beams

The simplest way of supporting a load across a gap is to use a beam – a horizontal structural member. The earliest types of bridges must have been formed by a tree falling across a river or stream. This accident of nature would have enabled people to cross over the water without getting wet, and also given people the idea of building simple beam bridges.

Fig. 4.128a

Bookshelves supported by brackets are simple beam structures. If they are over loaded with heavy books the shelf may bend in the middle. This problem can be solved in several ways. The shelf can be given more support by using another bracket placed near the middle, or the shelf itself can be made thicker or made a different shape.

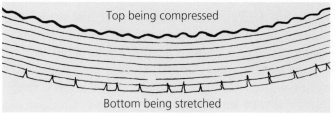

Top being compressed

Bottom being stretched

Fig. 4.128b

In Fig. 4.129, a load has been put on a wooden beam. The wood cannot support the forces acting on it and begins to bend. However, if the wood is turned on its edge, the beam is much stronger and resists bending (see Fig. 4.129). This is because a beam's resistance to bending is greatly increased if its top surface and bottom surface are moved further apart. Some beams even have holes in them and yet they are still very strong. A thicker beam is more rigid than a thin one, but it would be too expensive to always use thick solid beams. They would also be very heavy. Today most beams are made of steel.

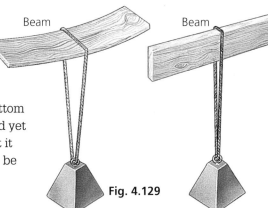

Beam

Beam

Fig. 4.129

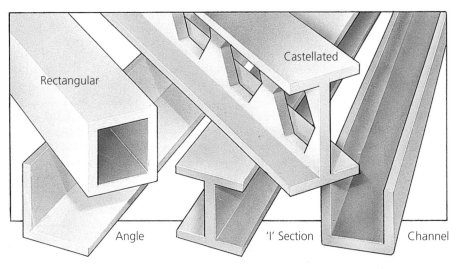

Rectangular

Castellated

Angle

'I' Section

Channel

Fig. 4.130 *Different types of steel beam used in construction*

Fig. 4.130 shows some different shapes and sections that are used to make strong, but light beams. They are examples of the different types of steel beam used in construction. You can see that they all use the edge-on principle. They are all very strong, but weigh and cost much less than a solid beam. The Britannia Railway Bridge, shown in Fig. 4.131, was designed by Robert Stephenson and built in 1850. The bridge was made from hollow, box-shaped beams, large enough to allow whole trains to pass through the inside (Fig. 4.132).

Fig. 4.131 *The Britannia Railway Bridge, trains passed through box beams.*

Fig. 4.132

Cantilevers ➡

Cantilevers are beams that are held and supported at one end only – for example, shelf brackets and hanging basket brackets (Fig. 4.133). Sometimes bridges that may look like beam or arched bridges are really two cantilevers that meet in the middle. Many concrete bridges used on motorways are built in this way.

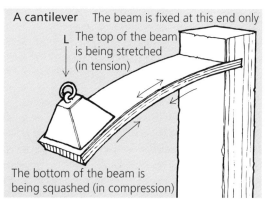

A cantilever   The beam is fixed at this end only

The top of the beam is being stretched (in tension)

The bottom of the beam is being squashed (in compression)

Fig. 4.134

Fig. 4.133

Fig. 4.135

Columns ⬅

Columns (and pillars) are vertical beams. They are normally designed to support loads directly on top – for example, chair legs and street lamps. Columns are also used to support the roofs of buildings. The Greeks were the first to use columns in this way when they built huge temples such as the Parthenon in Athens (see Fig. 4.135).

Arched and suspension bridges ➡

Arched bridges made from stone or brick have been used since Roman times. They are very strong. When blocks (or bricks) are arranged in a semi-circle to form an arch they can withstand a great weight from above. However, the arch must have rigid support to prevent the ends from spreading apart.

Suspension bridges also have a long history. They are called suspension bridges because the deck is supported from above by cables or chains which are attached to towers. The deck is therefore suspended.

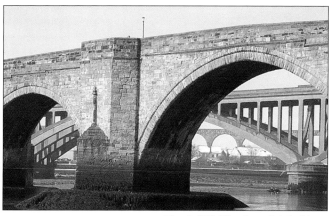

Fig. 4.136 *The Berwick bridges*

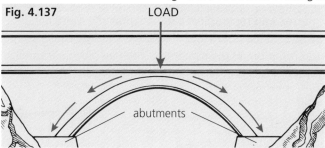

Fig. 4.137   LOAD

abutments

In arched bridges the load is transferred to the bridge supports (abutments). This is a compressive force.

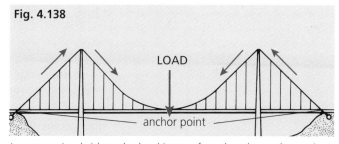

Fig. 4.138

LOAD

anchor point

In suspension bridges the load is transferred to the anchor points of the cables. This is a tensile force.

Fig. 4.139 *The San Francisco Bay Suspension Bridge*

Stabilising structures ➡

A stable structure is one that is safe and will not collapse. There are several ways of making structures more stable. Look at the stool in Fig. 4.140 that the elephant is standing on. The force on the stool (caused by the elephant's weight) makes the bottom of the legs move outwards. The stool is unstable. It can be made more stable by adding a bottom rail . Many stools and chairs have such a rail. The rail is being stretched in order to keep the stool stable. It is in tension. The stability of the stool depends upon the way that the rail is fixed into the legs, and the joints and glue used.

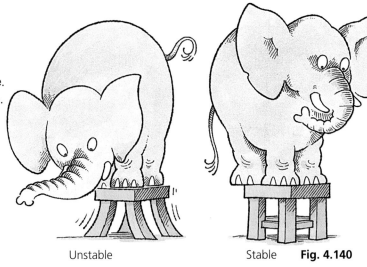

Unstable   Stable   **Fig. 4.140**

You may have seen decorators' step ladders that use a rope in tension to make them stable and safe (see Fig. 4.141). Rope is very good in tension. The advantage of rope in this situation is that the steps can be folded away after use. Structural members used in tension do not need to be stiff.

Fig. 4.142 *Triangulated structures*   **Fig. 4.141**

Triangulation

Instead of a rope, many step ladders today use the top platform to stop the two sides separating. When the platform is fixed in position the step ladder will not open or close. This is because the two sides and the platform form a triangle. Even with jointed angles, the shape of a triangle cannot be changed or squashed. All other shapes, including squares and rectangles, can be squashed more easily. But by adding one or more additional members and creating a triangle these shapes become stable. This is called triangulation. Many structures such as bicycle frames, shelf brackets, house roofs and garden gates (Fig. 4.143) are triangulated.

Fig. 4.143

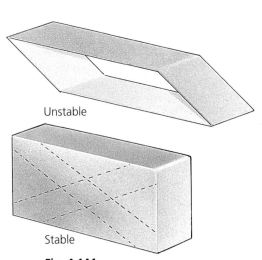

Unstable

Stable

Fig. 4.144

Unstable   Stable

If you are making a box out of card or wood, and you have joined together the four sides but not yet attached the bottom (or top), you will notice that the box is unstable and easily loses its shape. However, when you attach the bottom of the box, it will become stable and keep its shape. This is like adding cross members to form triangles, and then filling in the spaces. It is, in fact, a form of triangulation (see Fig. 4.144).

Check out your structures

1 Identify as many beams, cantilevers and columns as you can in and around your school. Find out from what material they are made, and how they are made.

2 Collect as many pictures of different types of bridge as you can. What factors do you think have influenced the way each bridge has been made? Is it the availability of materials, the cost of labour, the environment or some other factor?

Now let's have some fun!

These tasks use everyday materials. You can work on your own or in groups to see who can build the highest, strongest and most stable structure. You could also try them at home with your friends or family, but remember to clean up the mess when you've finished.

Fig. 4.145 *A primitive suspension bridge*

Fig. 4.146

Fig. 4.147 *Building a 'ballista'*

3 Each person (or group) will need 10 sheets of newspaper (make sure that the pieces of newspaper are all the same size), 100 mm of sticky tape, and a pair of scissors. Using just these materials, build the tallest self-supporting tower that you can. You may need a room with a high ceiling!

4 Using a single sheet of A4 paper, make a beam bridge that will support 0.5 kg over a 200 mm gap (Fig. 4.146). When you have completed your bridge, test it to see how much weight your bridge can support before it collapses.

5 You will need a piece of stiff card 150 mm square and some scissors. Without using any glue or sticky tape, and by only cutting the card into a maximum of 8 separate pieces, build a tower as tall as you can. It is a good idea to practise different ways of slotting or hooking together card before you start constructing your tower.

6 For this task you will need 20 drinking straws (you can cut them into short lengths if you wish), 12 paper clips (you can bend these but you must not cut them), and a hard-boiled egg. Using these materials build a three-legged structure to support the egg as far above the ground as possible. However, the three legs must be standing within a 100 mm diameter circle.

7 Using straws, dress-making pins and one elastic band, build a 'ballista'. (A ballista was an ancient catapult that was used for hurling stones at enemy fortifications.) The ballista should be able to catapult a table-tennis ball 6 metres to land, without bouncing, in a waste-paper basket.

5 PRODUCTS & PRODUCT DESIGN

In industry, products are designed, made and sold in order to earn money and create wealth. If you live in a country that can do this successfully, you can expect to enjoy a high standard of living with, for instance, good hospitals, schools, housing and roads. In school, products are designed and made as part of your D&T activities.

Fig. 5.1 *Modern manufacturing*

Manufacturing

People have designed and made things since they first learnt to work with materials thousands of years ago. At first, people made products for their own use, but they soon began to trade or sell them. Gradually, people began to work together to make things in what became known as 'cottage industries'.

With the development of new technology in the eighteenth century, steam power and new machinery meant that products could now be manufactured on a large scale. The Industrial Revolution in the United Kingdom formed the basis of modern manufacturing industries throughout the world.

Fig. 5.2 *Manufacturing during the Industrial Revolution*

Fig. 5.3 *Products are usually developed as a result of demand pull or technology push*

Demand pull

There must be a need or a demand for a product if it is to be successful. The development of products in response to this is referred to as the 'demand pull'. While there is a demand for a product from customers, new and improved products will be designed to meet their requirements.

Technology push

Products are also designed to make use of new technology. Old products are redesigned or updated to enable them to benefit from technological developments. This can be seen in the development of many products found in the home. Radios, televisions, vacuum cleaners, sewing machines and telephones (Fig. 5.4) have all been developed as technology has changed over a number of years. This is known as the 'technology push' because new technology 'pushes' forward the design of a product.

Developing a new product

Products are usually developed as a result of demand pull or technology push. The case study on pages 97 to 106 shows how a company identified an opportunity to produce a new range of products by targeting a particular section of the market.

Fig. 5.4 *The design development of the telephone*

Case study – Berol Ltd

You are probably familiar with some of the products produced by Berol Ltd. For many years they have produced pencils and pens for use in schools. The Eagle Pencil Company was originally founded in 1856 by Alfred Berol, and since then several other pencil companies have been taken over by the firm. In 1971 Eagle acquired the Venus Pencil Company and the new company became known as Berol Ltd.

Fig. 5.5 *The Berol offices in Kings Lynn*

Background

For many years Berol have been a major supplier of pencils and pens for schools but they have only done a limited amount of business in the graphics and art materials market. Berol decided to develop their products to meet the requirements of graphic designers and artists. In order to do this a design company called Newell and Sorrell was employed to develop and launch a new range of graphic products.

Fig. 5.6 *A range of Berol products*

The design process

The design process used in school is a framework to help you to learn how to design things. Professional designers do not always follow this exactly, they develop it to suit the way they work and the product that they are designing.

The design brief ➡

Discussions took place about exactly what was required (Fig. 5.7) and the following design brief was given to the designers:

'To enter the graphics market with a fully integrated, branded, visually attractive range of consumable products and materials and to achieve a significant market share in three years.'

At this point in a project in school, having set the task, you are required to analyse the situation, identify the problems that need to be addressed and compile a detailed specification. At Berol the designers followed a 'creative strategy'.

Fig. 5.7 *Discussions taking place between Berol staff and designers*

The creative strategy

Instead of drawing up a detailed specification, the designers established a 'creative strategy'. This was to influence the design of the whole project and carry through from products to packaging and on to merchandising and promotional material. The creative strategy had three principles: visual excellence, fitness for purpose and uniqueness. All parts of the product including the packaging had to fit all three of these principles. In this situation the creative strategy is very similar to a design specification but with not quite as much detail.

The creative strategy

Visual excellence	Fitness for purpose	Uniqueness

Product	Packaging	Marketing

Fig. 5.8 *A diagrammatic representation of the creative strategy*

Market research

Market research involves collecting information from people, recording it and making sense of it. It is carried out for two main reasons – to find out the demand for products or services, and to find out what will persuade people to buy or use them.

Before a product can be successfully marketed the following questions need to be considered:

- Who is the target market for the product? Depending on the nature of the product you may have to consider who will buy it, their age, sex, social background and where they live.
- What do people want? What do they like or dislike about a product – its design, quality, colour etc?
- What is the competition for your product? What is currently available on the market?

Check List

1. Target market

2. What do people want?

3. What is the competition?

Fig. 5.9 *A market research checklist*

Target market ➡

As Berol already had successful products in the commercial and educational markets it was felt that the new range of products should be targeted towards the graphics and art materials markets in Europe and the UK. It was decided that a range of products should be produced that would be used in design studios, drawing offices and art schools.

Customer requirements

Professional artists and designers require a range of graphic materials including different types of pencils, coloured pencils and markers. It was felt that if the products were to be successful they would have to appeal to the users.

Frances Newell, Creative Director at Newell and Sorrell, explains:

> 'The really important consideration was to appeal to the people who would be working with the products – illustrators, artists, designers, architects, draftsmen, students and so on. These people are visually aware, they are interested in what things look like, how they work and feel in use. So the colours and styling of the packaging need not be strident or garish to be understood, and attention to detail would be important to them.'

Fig. 5.10 *Berol wanted to target professional designers and artists*

Fig. 5.11

Developing the designs

The designers felt that the whole range of products should all be developed at the same time rather than individually. The packaging was seen as an essential part of the product and was developed alongside the products as part of the overall design. The principles of visual excellence, fitness for purpose and uniqueness set out in the creative strategy on page 98 also included the packaging and marketing as well as the products themselves. Rather than developing a design for the products and then designing the packaging, the designers worked on both at the same time using the same design specification.

Fig. 5.12 *Products in the Karisma range*

⬅ *The competition*

In producing products for this market, Berol are in direct competition with the other major manufacturers of graphics equipment and so it was particularly important to look at the products available. In terms of coloured pencils, all of the existing competitive products available had two things in common; the pencils themselves had a paint finish to an approximate colour match for the leads, and they were all packaged in bright metal boxes (Fig. 5.11).

Pencils

Each of the products in the range, which was to be known as the 'Karisma' range, would be very different from each other. They would perform different functions and be made from different materials. The first of the Karisma products to be developed was a range of pencils. This included water soluble drawing pencils, a range of 72 coloured pencils, and dense blacklead drawing pencils. Instead of painting the pencils to match the lead colour and putting them into bright metal boxes, Newell and Sorrell recommended a more sensitive approach. *'Pencils have a long history'*, said Frances Newell. *'They have been used since 1795. We have all grown up using them at home, at school, at work. They are part of everyday life. Because of this they have a certain nostalgic quality. They are also pleasing to use – wood is a good material to feel, it has beautiful natural colours, and smells pleasant.'*

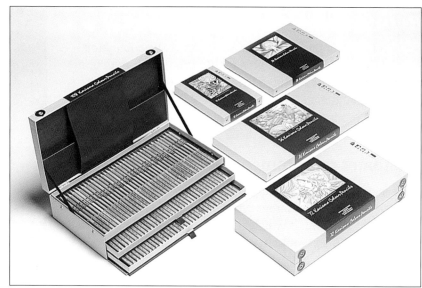

Fig. 5.13 *Karisma colour pencils*

Fig. 5.14 *The chamfered ends of the Karisma colour pencils*

It was decided, therefore, to make use of the properties and qualities of natural wood in the design of the pencils. Instead of painting the casing of the pencils they were left unpainted to allow the natural colour of the wood to be seen and enjoyed. However, this did create a problem for the designers to solve. How would people be able to identify one colour of pencil from another when working with them?

The solution that was arrived at was a major change from traditional pencil design. It was suggested that the end of each pencil could be cut off at an angle (chamfered) so that the lead was exposed at the end as well as at the tip. This enabled the user to see the exact colour of the lead.

Markers

Compared with the pencil the marker is a relatively new product and so a less traditional approach was taken with the design of the Karisma double-ended markers. A functional and practical design was developed which allowed each marker to combine a thin and thick tip, so that detailed lines and broad washes could be made with each marker. The system was designed to save both space and time and to appeal to users working in a range of different graphic styles.

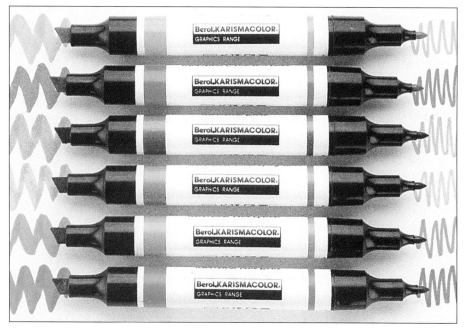

Fig. 5.15 *Karisma double-ended markers*

Packaging

Pencils

The packaging for the Karisma products is very important in selling the products. The products in the range are not new or unique to Berol and all of their competitors produce very similar products. The packaging, therefore, had to create a quality image and encourage people to buy the products. The designers got much of their inspiration for the packaging of the pencils from looking at traditional artists' equipment and stationery products. These products use a range of materials including canvas, wood and metal, and have incorporated details such as paper document ties, metal eyelets and paper binders.

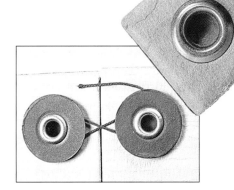

Fig. 5.16 *Traditional artists' equipment inspired the designers of the Karisma pencils' packaging*

The outside of the boxes were wrapped in textured, recycled paper, in different colours to identify each of the pencil types. A soft grey/blue paper was used for the 'Aquarelle' pencils (water-soluble graphite pencils), greenish buff for the coloured pencils and a soft grey for the blacklead pencils. Brass eyelets, hinges and document ties are used as finishing details on the larger boxes (Fig. 5.17).

Fig. 5.17 *Document ties and brass eyelets – some of the finishing details used on the Karisma packaging*

Fig. 5.18 *The traditional silver hallmark, a guarantee of quality*

Fig. 5.19 *Hallmarks on Karisma boxes*

Identifying the products on the outside of the boxes was another problem for the designers to solve. They did not want to spoil the traditional look of the boxes by printing the product information on the lids. The solution was to print all the information on a separate band of paper which was then wrapped around the lid (Fig. 5.13). The paper is then removed when the pencils are unwrapped and used for the first time. In order to identify the products when they are unwrapped, Newell and Sorrell designed a series of hallmarks that could be embossed on the lids. Traditionally, hallmarks are used on silver as a guarantee of its quality (Fig. 5.18). On the Karisma products they also suggest quality as well as giving information about the products.

Markers

A very different approach was taken with the packaging of the markers. They have been packed in sleek modern vacuum-formed plastic boxes which continue the theme of practical and functional graphics equipment. The plastic boxes can be kept and used as storage cases for the markers. Modern materials have been used in a subtle way to suggest quality products. They provide a direct contrast to the pencils in the Karisma range which rely on the use of traditional materials to do the same thing.

Fig. 5.20 *The packaging for the double-ended markers*

Manufacturing

Pencils

The process of making what has been designed, from raw materials to finished product, is known as manufacturing. Pencil manufacturing is an international industry which brings raw materials together from different parts of the world and then sends out its finished products all over the world.

The pencil 'leads' are made of a mixture of a natural mineral known as graphite and clay which is mixed together and then fired in ovens to produce a strong fused stick. Berol use graphite from Mexico and clay from Bavaria in Germany. The graphite and clay are mixed together in varying proportions. The proportions determine the hardness or softness of the pencil. The more graphite that is used, the softer and blacker the pencil will be.

The casing for the 'lead' is made of wood, usually Californian cedar. The wood is sawn into slats, each six or seven pencils wide and then seasoned. It is then run through a grooving machine and the grooves are impregnated with a resinous bonding material to prevent the wood from splitting. The graphite and clay sticks are laid in the grooves and a second grooved slat is glued on the top and pressed together to form a sandwich. The sandwiches are then fed into a moulding machine which forms them into individual pencils. The pencils are then ready for finishing which involves giving them several coats of lacquer and hot foil stamping them with the brand name and grade and then finally sharpening them. Coloured pencils are manufactured in exactly the same way as graphite pencils except that they are not fired in an oven but carefully dried for long periods in air conditioned rooms before being made into sandwiches.

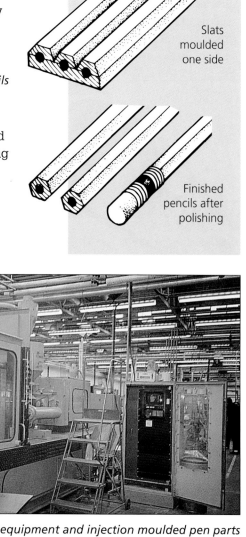

Cedarwood slat

Slats grooved ready to receive lead

Slats with lead prior to moulding

Slats moulded one side

Finished pencils after polishing

Fig. 5.21 *The stages involved in making pencils*

Markers

The main parts of markers, the body, cap, end plug and barrel are produced using a manufacturing process known as injection moulding. Thermosetting plastics such as polythene, polypropylene and ABS are heated to approximately 280°C, mixed with pigments to colour them and then injected under pressure into steel moulds. Injection moulding is an expensive process and to make the most economic use of the machinery multi-cavity moulds are used. The largest of these moulds is capable of producing 64 marker pen parts every 18 to 25 seconds. The moulding machines at the Berol manufacturing plant operate for 24 hours a day on a 3-shift system.

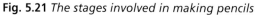

Fig. 5.22 *Injection moulding equipment and injection moulded pen parts*

The inks used in the markers are manufactured by Berol but the tips and the ink reservoirs are bought from other companies. The company which makes the reservoirs also makes filter tips for most of the cigarette companies around the world.

The markers are assembled by a specially designed pen assembly machine which can put together 40,000 pens per day. In manufacturing terms the process of making things in large quantities like this is known as mass production. Berol produces about one and half million writing instruments every week.

Fig. 5.23 The Berol pen assembly machines at Kings Lynn

Fig. 5.24 Quality control at Berol

← *Quality assurance*

It is the responsibility of designers and manufacturers to ensure that their products are of the highest standards in terms of design, manufacture and fitness for purpose. Most products must meet UK and worldwide safety standards before they can be sold.

Quality control in industry

Quality control is taken very seriously by most manufacturers. At Berol raw materials of all types have to pass rigorous quality checks on arrival at the factories. Most materials pass the tests first time because they come from specialist suppliers who know exactly what Berol require. Quality control is maintained throughout the manufacturing processes carried out within the company. Machine operators are expected to be inspectors and check the products that they produce. The pen assembly machines check after each operation to see that it has been carried out successfully and faulty products are automatically ejected. In addition, there are also patrol inspectors who make random spot checks, checking first-off production and final batch inspection.

The final inspection is carried out by dividing the products into batches of up to 10,000 pieces and then taking a random sample of 200. Each of these 200 products is carefully examined for faults. If faults are found they are classified into critical, major and minor categories. A critical fault is usually one which makes the product useless to the purchaser while minor faults are ones which the customer probably would not notice, such as an end cap not fully pushed into the barrel. If one of the 200 sample shows a critical fault, then the whole of the 10,000 batch will be inspected.

Fig. 5.25 One of Berol's pen testing machines

Marketing

Marketing is about making sure that people want to buy what you are selling, and making sure that you are producing what people want to buy. Selling a product is not as simple as it may seem. Serious thought has to be given to how the product will be advertised, where it will be sold and what it will cost. When Newell and Sorrell designed the Karisma range for Berol many of these things were thought about at the design stage of the project. Marketing was included in their original creative strategy (specification). The key points of marketing are sometimes referred to as the '4Ps' as shown in Fig. 5.26. Thinking of it in this way helps us to understand what is known as 'the marketing mix'.

Fig. 5.26 *The marketing mix*

Point of sale material

Fig. 5.27 shows some of the point of sale material that Newell and Sorrell designed to help to market the Karisma range.

Fig. 5.27 *The Karisma pencil merchandiser*

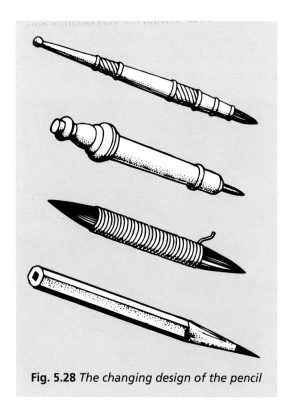

Fig. 5.28 *The changing design of the pencil*

Evaluating products

Evaluating in industry

When Newell and Sorrell designed the Karisma range for Berol they had the opportunity to develop a new product range in order to attract new customers to the company. Industrial designers are usually involved in developing or redesigning existing products rather than creating new ones. The Karisma product range has become very successful for Berol and is on sale in over 700 outlets in the UK and exported to Europe, the USA and Japan. The task now is to monitor and evaluate the products to make sure that they are continuing to meet the customers needs. Successful products are constantly evaluated, and updated when necessary (Fig. 5.28). Changes to the designs may have to be made in the future due to one or more of the following:

- Falling sales
- Changing styles and fashions
- Incorporating new technology into the product
- Incorporating new technology into the manufacturing process
- Selling the product from a different angle (e.g. a manufacturer may decide to stress that an existing product is environmentally friendly to attract customers who are concerned about the environment)
- Competition from rival products – manufacturers need to keep ahead of their competitors in product design if they are to keep their share of the market

Evaluating an existing product

Your design activities in school do not have to begin with identifying needs. Evaluating a product or a system can provide you with many opportunities for designing. You may be asked to improve an existing product or to re-design it completely. Evaluating an existing product will enable you to learn a lot about designing. You can study how other designers have made use of the materials and the technology available to them when making their products.

You should begin to evaluate a product by studying it carefully and then trying to work out the designer's original aims. If possible draw up your own specification for the product and check against it if the product meets the original aims. It may be possible for you to test the product to find out how it was made and how well it works. Use the checklist shown in Fig. 5.29 to help you.

Once you have a good understanding of the product and its function, you can begin to suggest improvements that may be made. Sometimes a minor alteration can make a product more efficient or cheaper to manufacture.

Understanding Products

Making a careful study of products can lead to a greater understanding of their design, manufacture and the technology used.

Disassembly

An excellent way of finding out how a product works or how it is made is to take it apart. However, a word of caution is required at this point. Do not take apart anything without permission or without being told to do so. Several graphic techniques can be used to record the disassembly of products. They will be useful in helping you to reassemble the products and will provide you with a permanent record of your activities.

Exploded drawings

Exploded drawings (see page 23) are normally used to show how a product is assembled but they are also excellent for recording disassembly. Fig. 5.30 on the right shows an exploded drawing of a Berol colour marker. It shows all the component parts and also gives us some idea of how it works. Exploded drawings can be made using almost any 3-dimensional drawing method such as isometric, oblique or perspective. Exploded drawings are used in car repair and maintenance manuals to help with disassembly and re-assembly.

Checklist

1. What were the designer's original aims? Draw up what you think was their design specification

2. How well does the product meet the specification?

3. How well does the product work?

4. How well is the product made?

5. What materials have been used for the product? Are they suitable?

6. Is the product environmentally friendly?

7. What improvements to the product can you suggest?

Fig. 5.29 *Product design checklist*

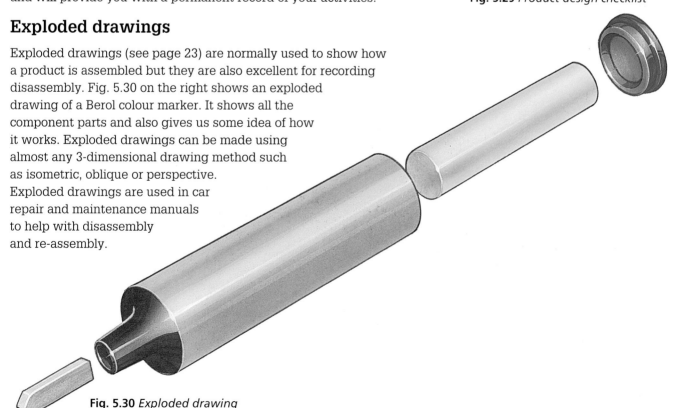

Fig. 5.30 *Exploded drawing of a Berol colour marker*

Section drawings

Sections (see page 23) are also useful when disassembling products because they show what an object looks like inside. Fig. 5.31 shows the same marker pen but this time it has been sectioned to show how it works.

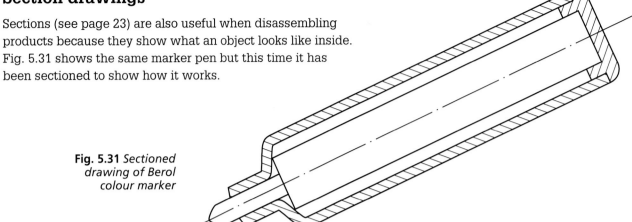

Fig. 5.31 *Sectioned drawing of Berol colour marker*

Identifying technological principles

Disassembling more complex products will enable you to identify the technological and scientific principles that have been used in their design. The use of materials can also been seen and you may be able to recognise them and suggest why certain types of material have been used for specific parts of the product.

Take care when taking products to pieces. Do not force them apart and take care not to damage anything. Some products, because of the way that they have been made, will not be able to be put back together again so make sure that you have permission to use them.

Never disassemble electrical products. Components inside them such as capacitors can still give electric shocks even when not connected to the mains.

Fig. 5.32 *A Berol pen – one complete and one disassembled*

Check out your product design

1 Choose a product that you are familiar with and then, using the checklist in Fig. 5.29 on page 105 evaluate it carefully and thoroughly.

2 Fig. 5.33 shows two very different products – a pair of 'Wonder Wipers' glasses and a ball pen. Look at them and think about each of them very carefully. Use the checklist on page 105 to evaluate them. Then answer the following questions:

   a) Which of the two products do you think will sell more (i) in the short term? and (ii) in the long term? Why?

   b) What technological problems do you think the designer of the wonder wipers might have?

   c) How might the ball pen be improved?

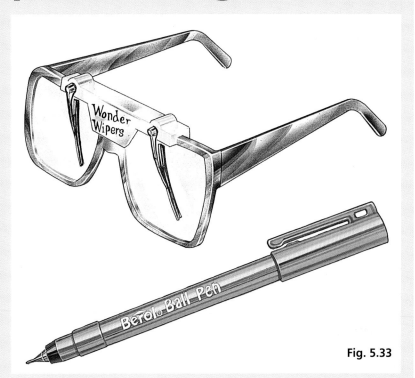

Fig. 5.33

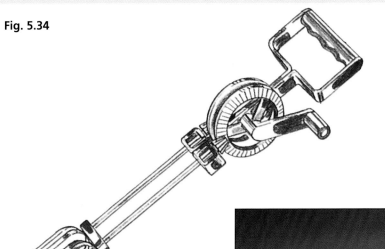

Fig. 5.34

3 Look at the hand whisk in Fig. 5.34. What technological principles do you recognise? List them and explain how the whisk works.

4 Make a list of the main things to consider when marketing a product.

5 Explain and discuss why designers and manufacturers are responsible for the products that they produce.

6 Explain what is meant by 'demand pull' and 'technology push'.

7 Fig. 5.35 shows Berol pens packaged and ready for sale.

   a) Explain the importance of packaging in product design

   b) List the main points that need to be considered when designing packaging for products.

Fig. 5.35

ACKNOWLEDGEMENTS

The publishers would like to thank the following for their help
in researching and providing material:

Val Elwell

John Storrs

Marion Ross at Berol Ltd

John Sorrel and Caroline Wilson at Newell and Sorrell

Mike Brown at Techsoft

For permission to reproduce photographs and illustrations:

ACCO UK (5.11)
Ace Photo Agency (4.1, 4.48)
Berol Ltd (5.5, 5.6, 5.7, 5.13, 5.15, 5.20, 5.21, 5.22, 5.23,
    5.24, 5.25, 5.27, 5.28, 5.32, 5.35)
Boxford Ltd (3.84)
Graham Bradbury (1.78, 4.42)
Britax (1.80)
British Standards Institution (1.74)
British Telecommunications plc (5.4 c, f, g)
BT Museum (5.4 a, b, d, e)
Colin Chapman (1.73, 3.3, 3.6, 3.52, 3.130)
Collections (4.136)
Colour-Rail (4.131)
Commotion (4.117)
Daler Rowney (5.16)
Data Harvest (4.118)
Draper Tools Ltd (3.2, 3.28, 3.29, 3.45)
Economatics (4.112, 4.116)
Graduate Lathe Company Ltd (3.82)
Sally and Richard Greenhill (1.3, 4.65)
Halfords Limited (4.44)
Hepworth Building Products (2.43)
Michael Horsley (3.23, 3.73, 3.74, 3.75, 3.77, 3.78, 3.85,
    4.83, 4.87, 4.92, 4.93)
IBM (1.79)
Illustrated London News (4.125)
Janome UK Ltd (4.6 right)
Peter Jennings (4.34)
Lego Dacta UK (4.46)

Littlewoods Organisation Ltd (2.38)
Longman Logotron (1.81)
Magnet plc (1.83)
Michael Manni Photographic (1.42)
Milepost 92$^1/_2$ (4.59, 4.60)
Patrick and Philippa Moyle (2.37, 4.28)
National Tourist Organisation of Greece (4.135)
Newell and Sorrell (5.12, 5.14, 5.17, 5.18, 5.19)
Mel Peace (2.33, 3.27)
Record Hand Tools (3.1, 3.79, 3.83)
Science Museum (5.2)
Science Photo Library (4.101, 4.110, 4.119, 4.120,
    4.123, 4.139)
Peter Sharp (1.11, 1.43, 1.59, 1.82)
Sony (5.3)
Stanley Tools (4.53)
Staübli Unimation (4.52)
Techsoft (1.84, 1.85, 1.86, 1.87, 3.86, 3.87, 3.88,
    3.89, 3.90)
Telegraph Colour Library (5.1, 5.10)
Topper International (3.68)
Unilab (4.47, 4.49, 4.64)
Alison Walters (4.113)
Bill Walters (4.142)
John Watney (4.67)
Charlotte and Lucy Watson (4.133)
Zanussi (4.6 left)
Zefa Pictures (2.21, 4.66, 4.121 left, 4.145)
ZF (4.37)

Note to teachers

Collins Design and Technology Foundation Course *is a new book built upon the sound tradition of the* CDT Foundation Course. *It has been written to suit National Curriculum Design and Technology at Key Stage 3 in the areas of resistant materials, systems and control, and structures. It includes up-to-date material on systems and control, and the chapter on products and product design provides a focus on designing and making in industry.*

Throughout the book you will find questions and exercises related to the material on the page, and safety issues are highlighted wherever they are relevant.

Be aware of safety. Look for this symbol:

The material in this book provides an ideal foundation for GCSE or Standard Grade. The complete requirements for GCSE and Standard Grade qualifications are met by the individual books in the *Collins Real-World Technology* series.

Graphic Products
Graphic Communication

Resistant Materials Technology
Craft and Design

Electronic Products
Electronics options in **Systems and Control Technology** and **Technological Studies**

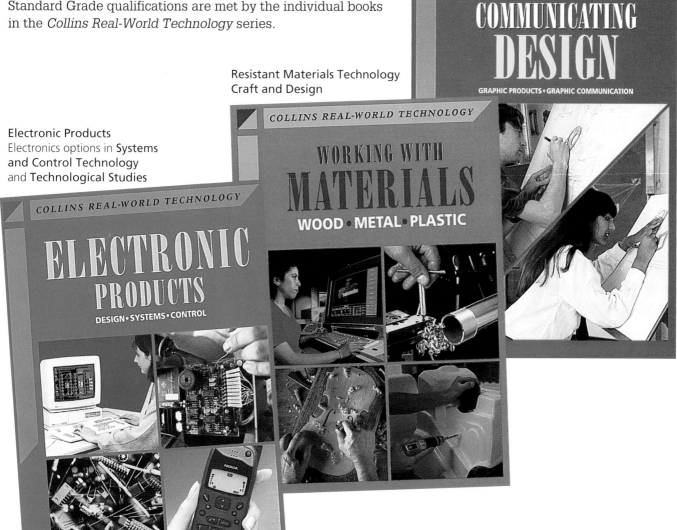

INDEX